Lines of Wisdom

Dr. Farzana Asim

Book Title: Lines of Wisdom
© 2021 by Dr. Farzana Asim

Published 2021
ISBN: 978-616-586-888-4

To My Children
Farheen and Zaigham
You continue to energize me and make me stronger than I ever imagined

PREFACE

Continuous line art dates to the early 20th century, starting with Pablo Picasso. He took complex, realistic ideas and simplified them into one unbroken line. I am carrying on that beautiful style. But my drawings are different; in my art, I try to capture ideas that resonate with life and speak to our experiences as humans. After all, what is the point of art if it doesn't help people, if it doesn't evoke emotion, if it doesn't challenge one's thinking?

I love single-line drawings as a medium because they force you to focus on the visual essentials. Therefore, my digital continuous line art is focused on capturing the unique characteristics of the subjects with as much simplicity as possible. I keep my line art consistent by ensuring that the line has one consistent thickness, only curved turns, and a beginning and an end. It is as minimal as possible.

I invite you to walk with me through the inky road of my thoughts, guided by a steady hand. This book will be our first milestone with many more to come.

Dr. Farzana Asim

Table of Contents

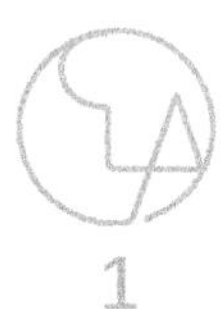

1

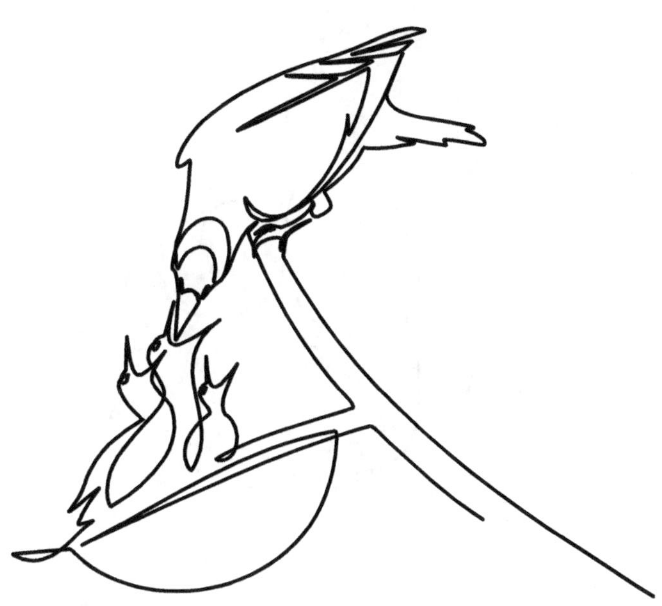

Love Unconditionally

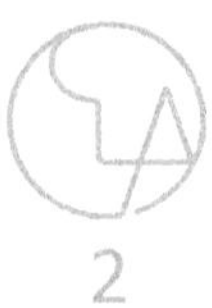

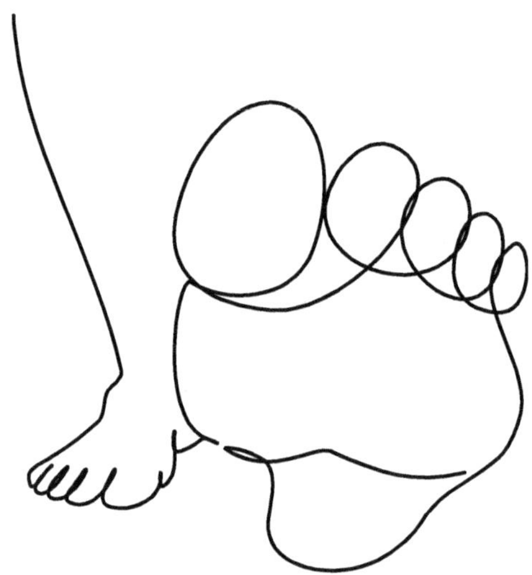

Walk Your Own Path

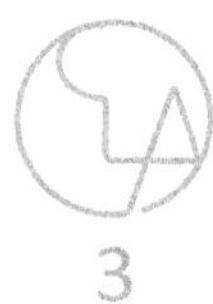

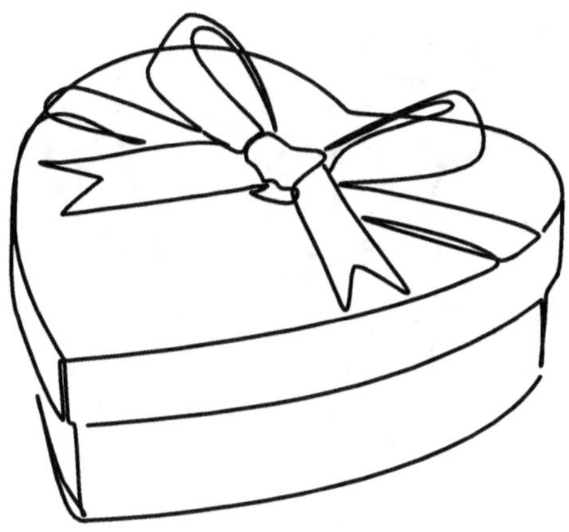

Follow Your Heart

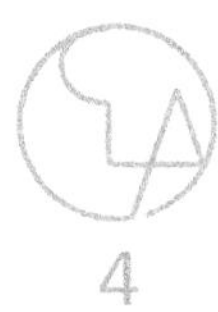

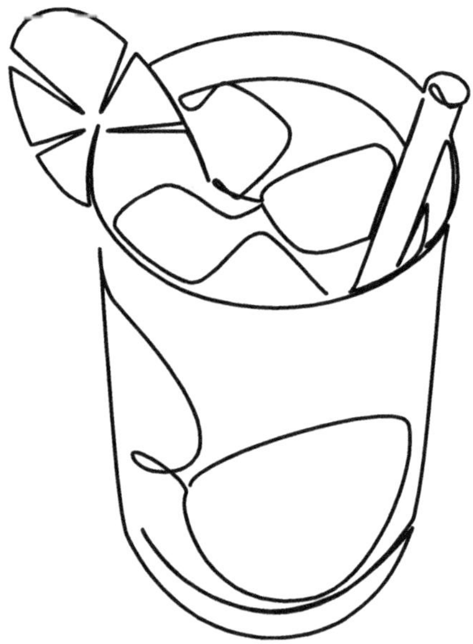

When Life Gives You Lemons, Make Lemonade

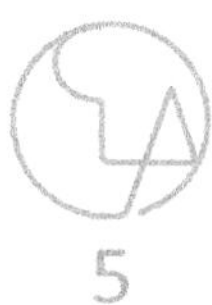

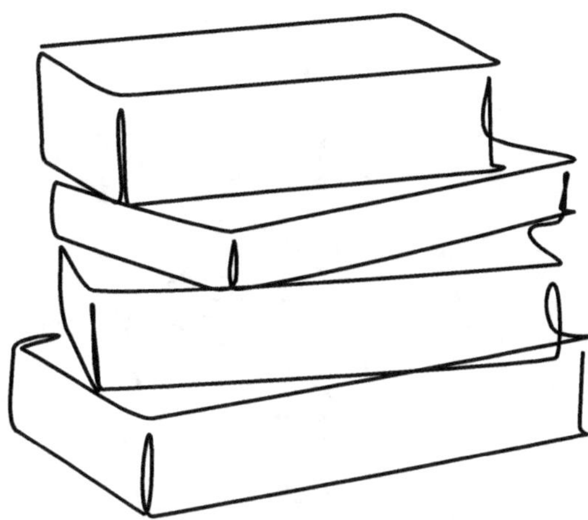

Don't Just Learn, Experience

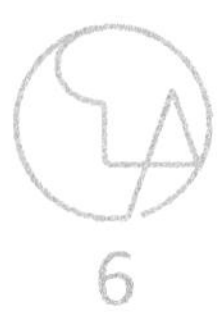

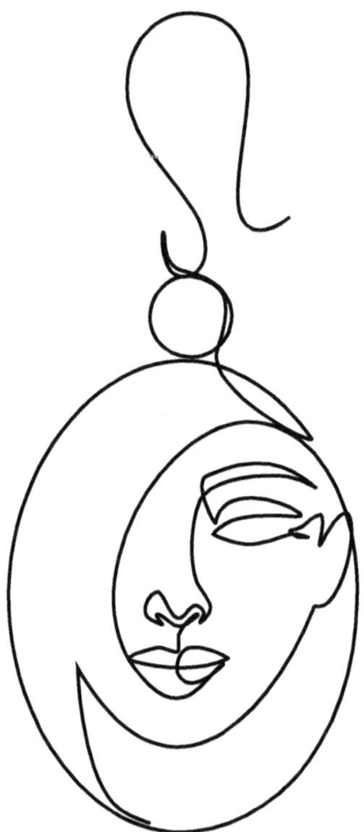

Beauty Lies in Your True Self

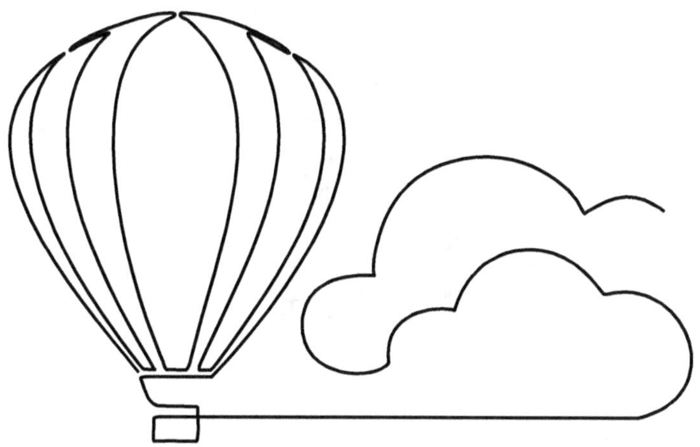

Savor the Journey

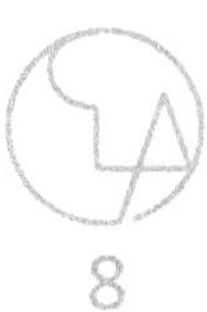

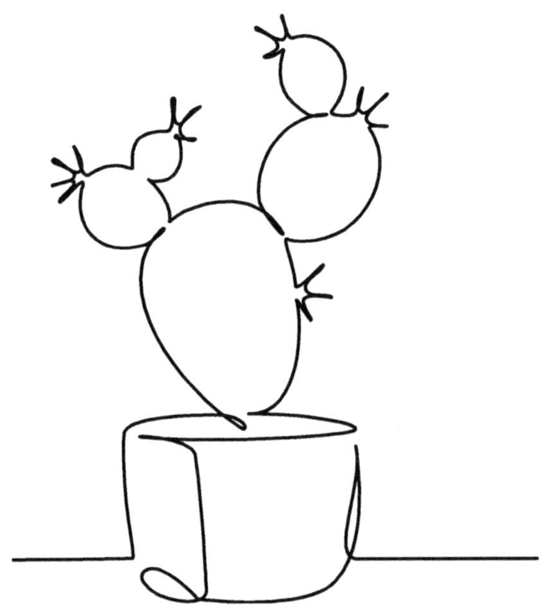

Be Your Own Kind of Beautiful

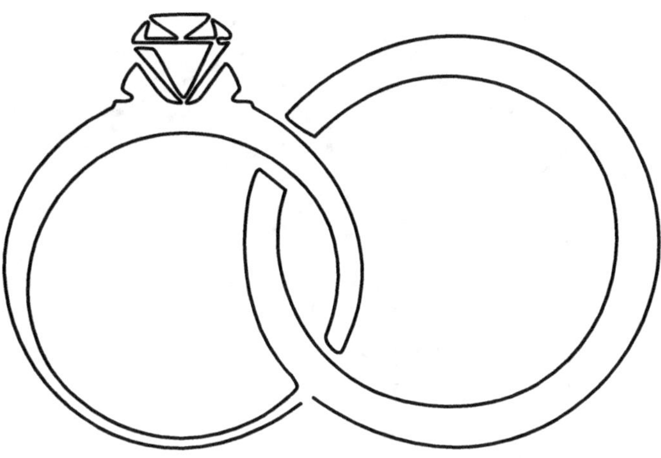

Love Is Meant to Nurture, Not Enslave

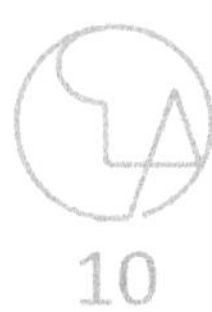

10

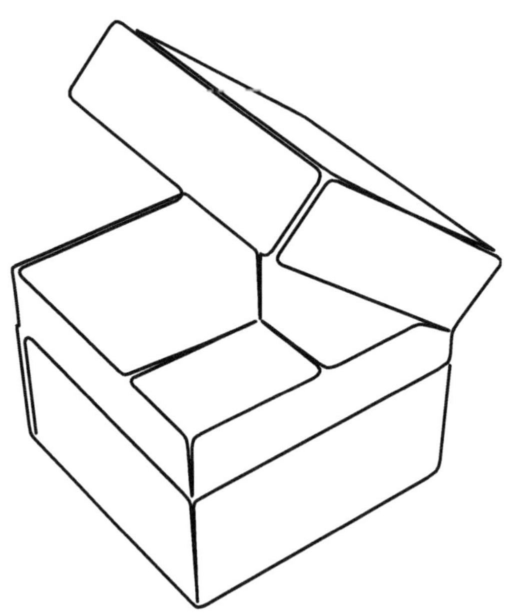

Open Yourself Up to New Ideas

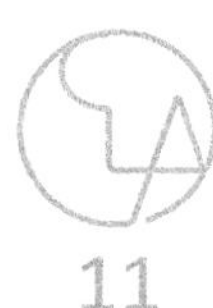

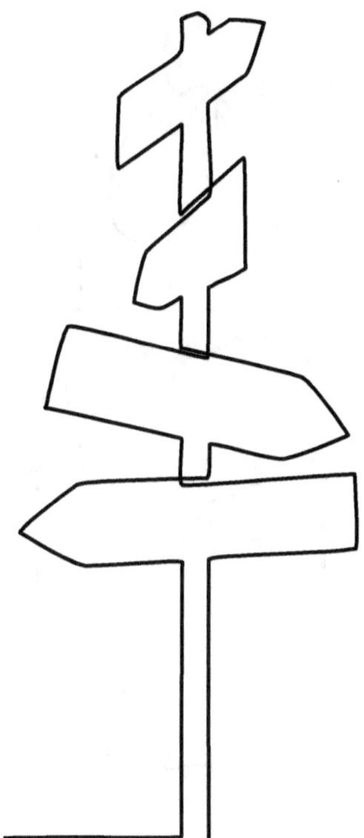

Follow Your Own Path

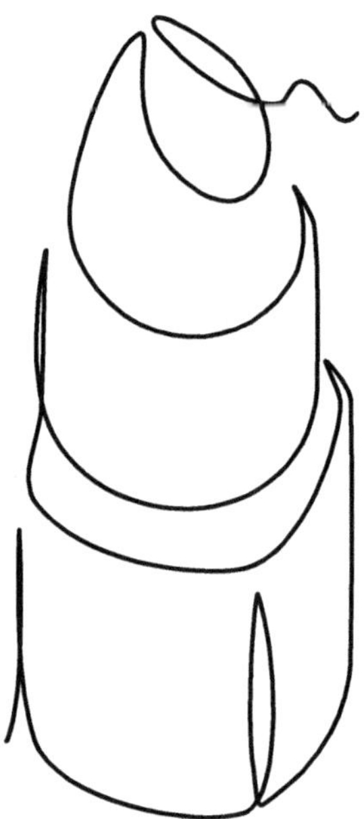

Let Your Natural Beauty Shine

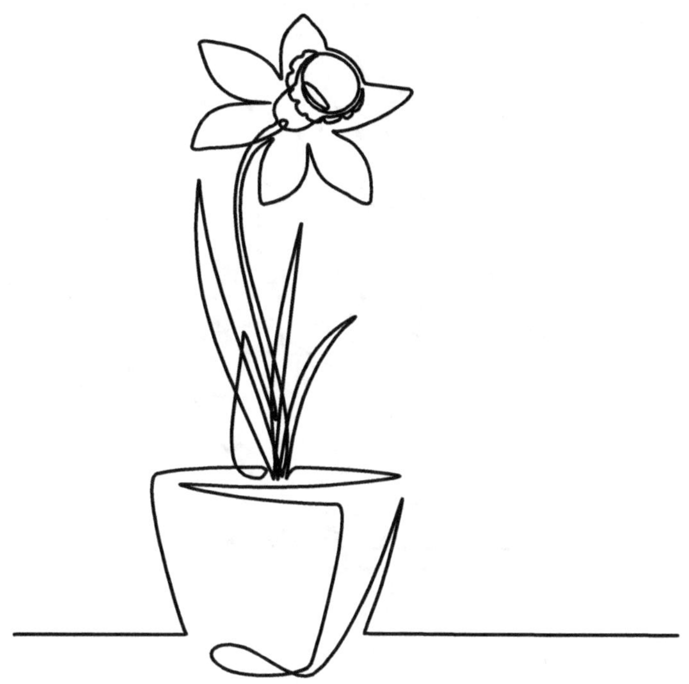

Bloom Where You're Planted

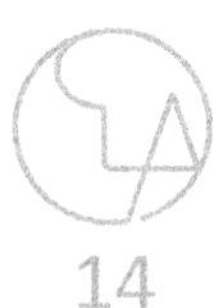

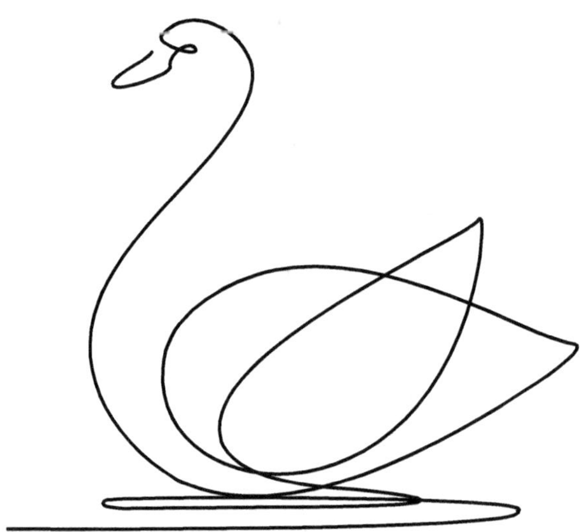

Live in Grace

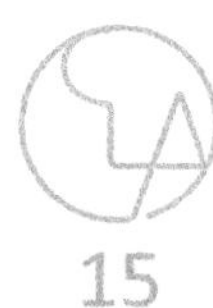

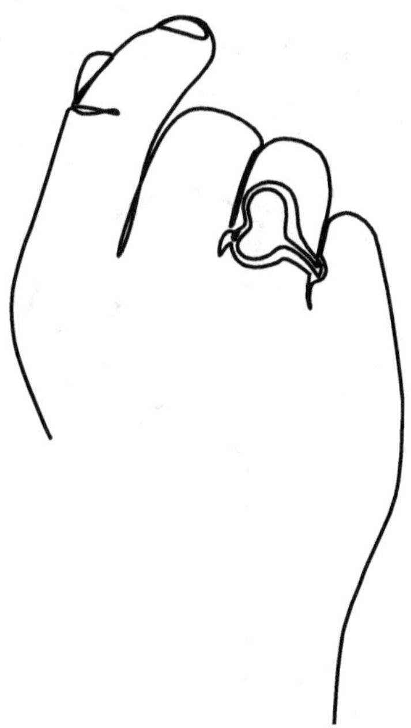

Be the Reason Someone Feels Loved

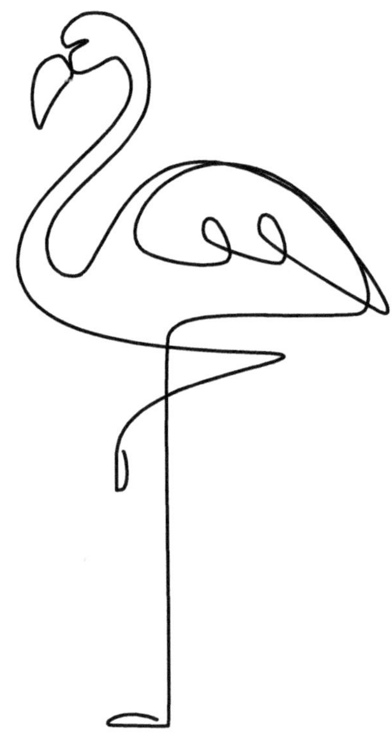

The Best Way to Relax Is to Do What You Love

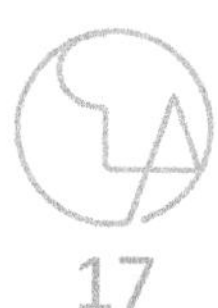

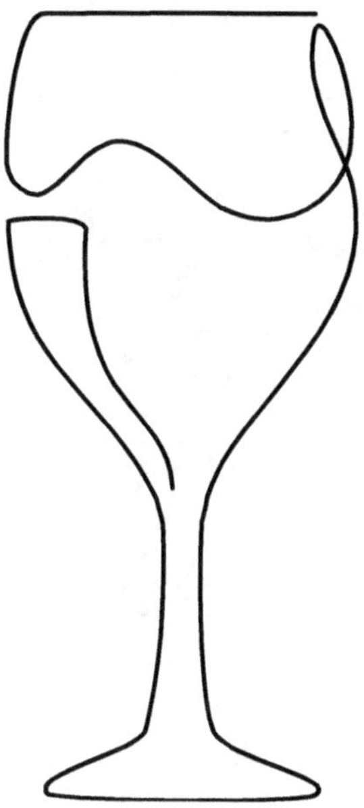

Count Your Blessings

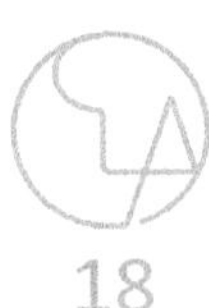

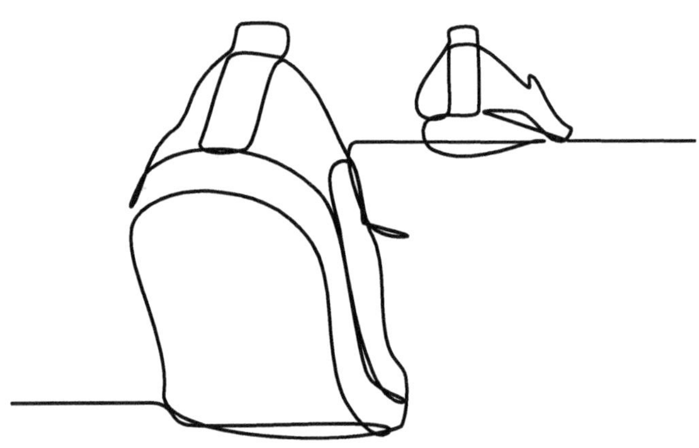

Take the Harder Path

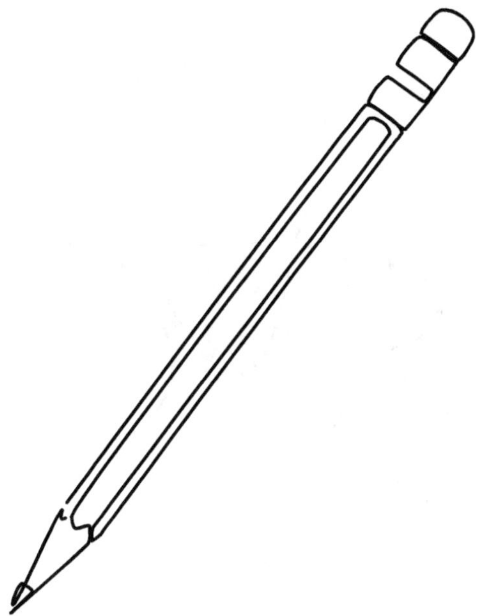

No One Is Flawless

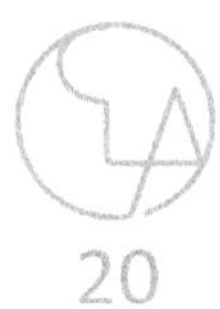

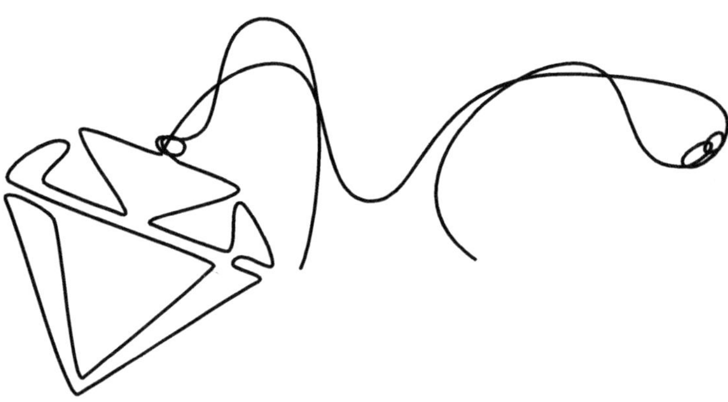

Relationships Never Die a Natural Death

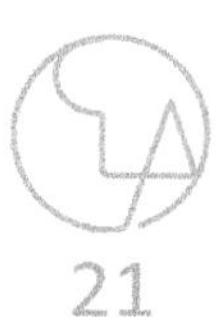

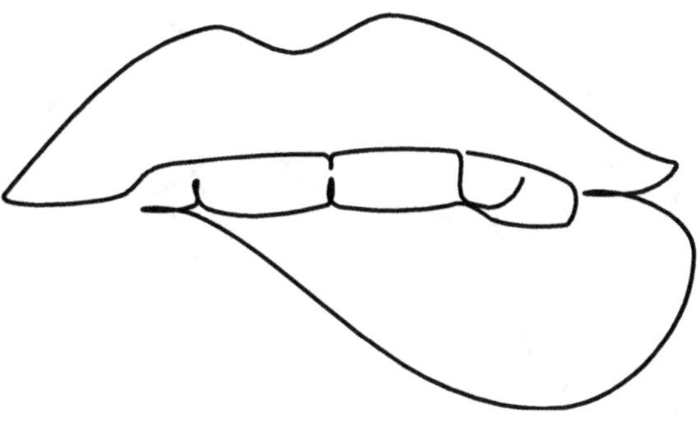

Love the Soul

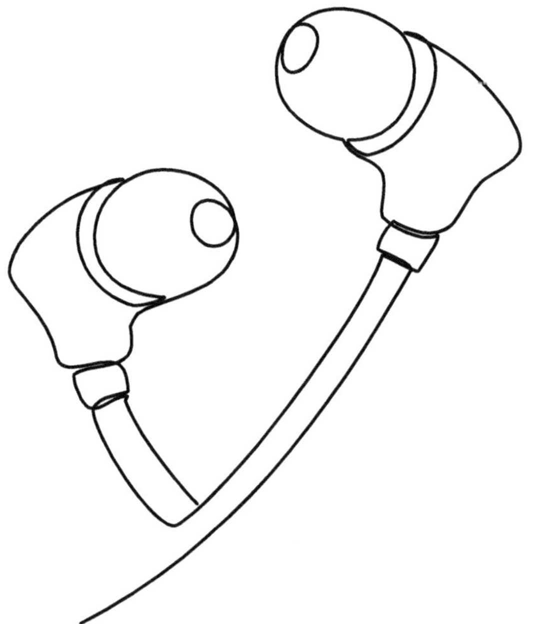

Find Your Rhythm and Stick to It

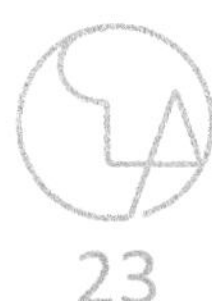

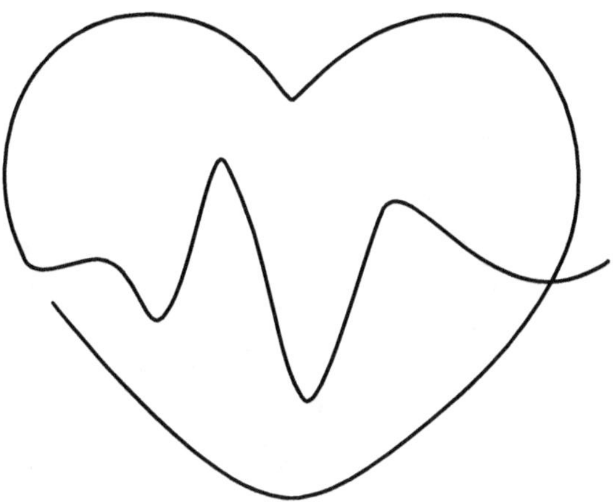

The Ups and Downs of Life Help Us Grow

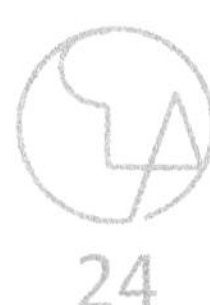

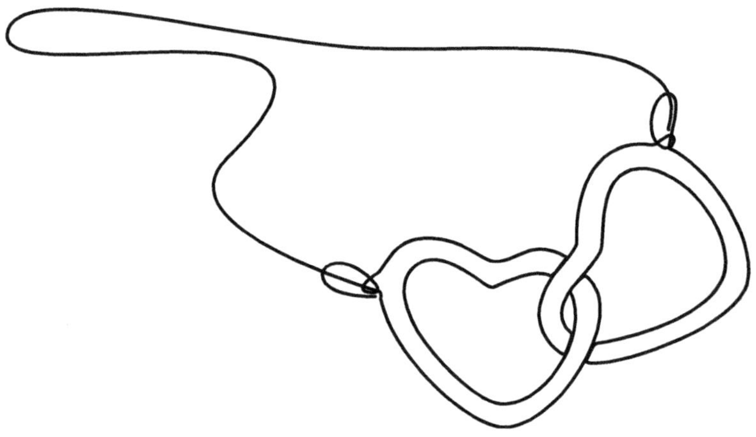

Be With Someone Who makes You a Better Person

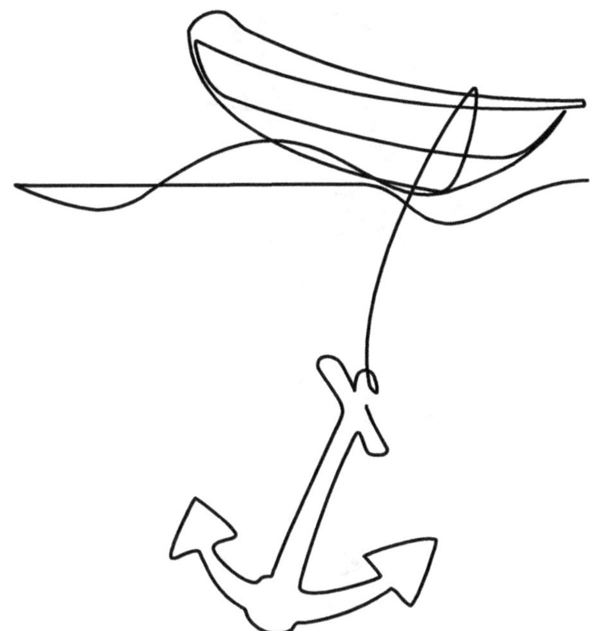

Never Let Anyone's Jealousy Drag You Down

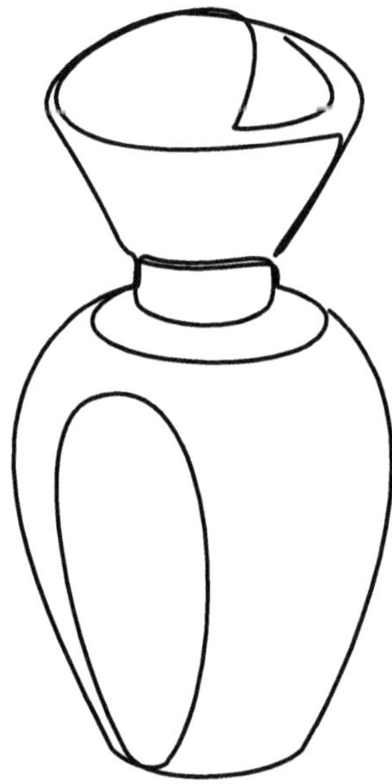

Fragrance Speaks for Itself

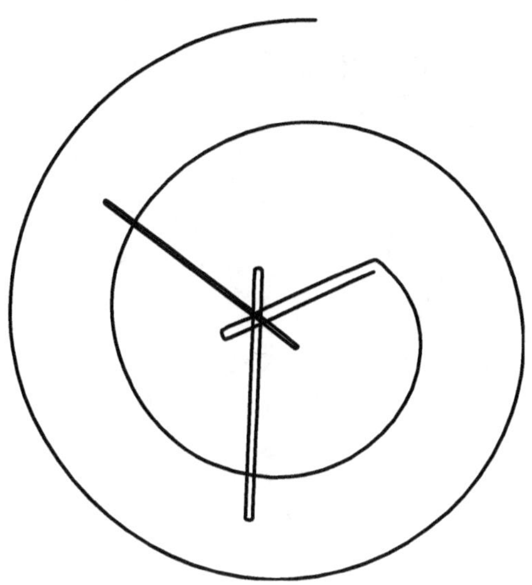

Be the Master of Your Time

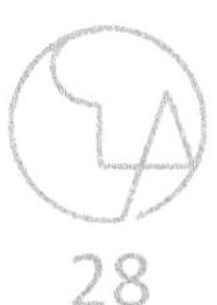

28

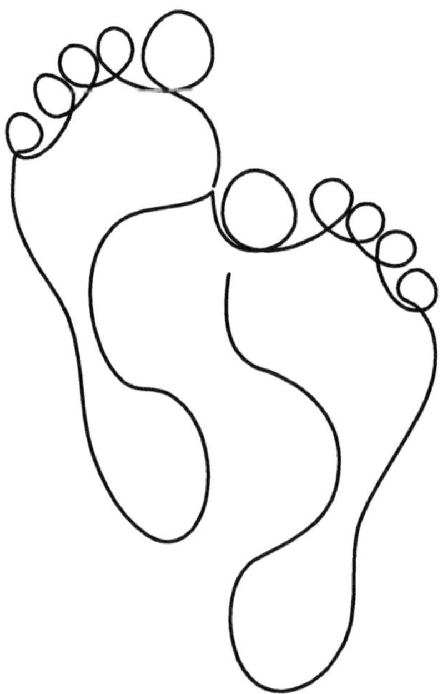

Leave Your Mark

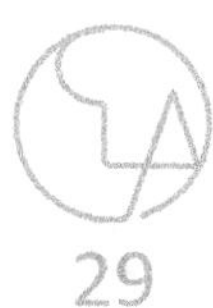

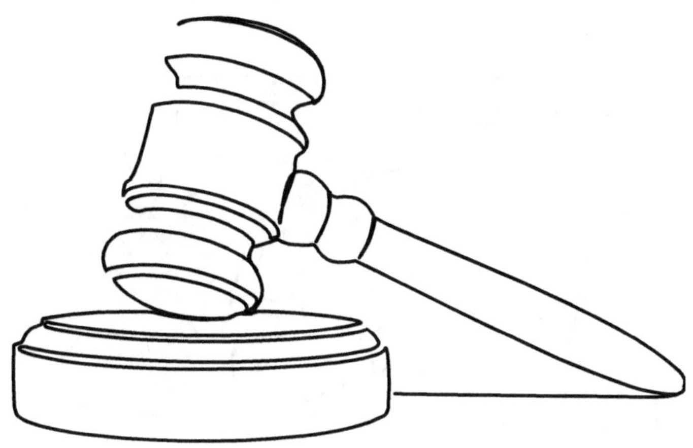

Question Your Beliefs

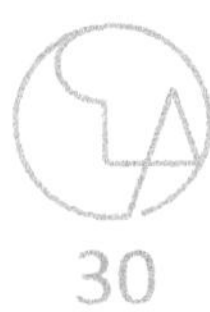

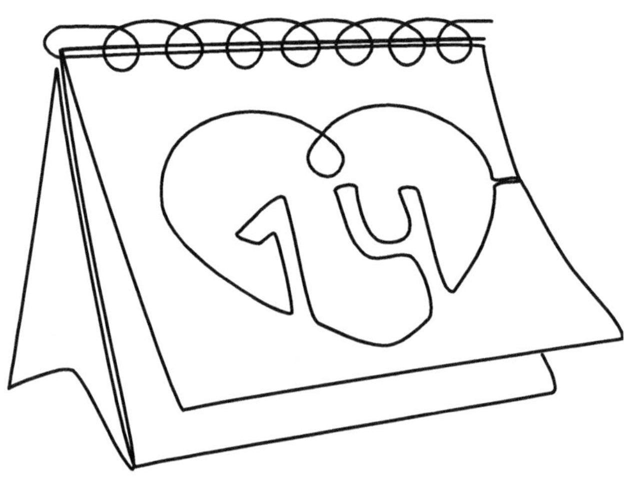

Make Every Moment Matter

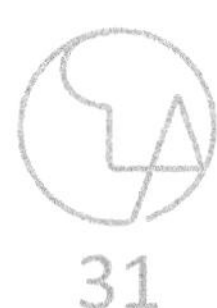

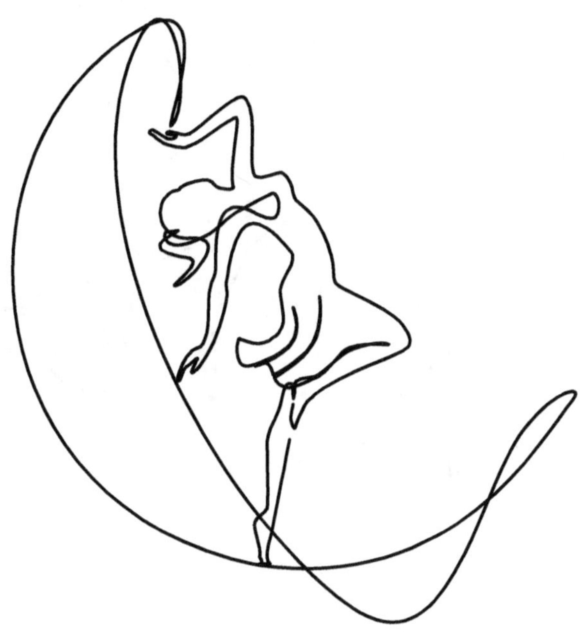

Dance Your Own Dance

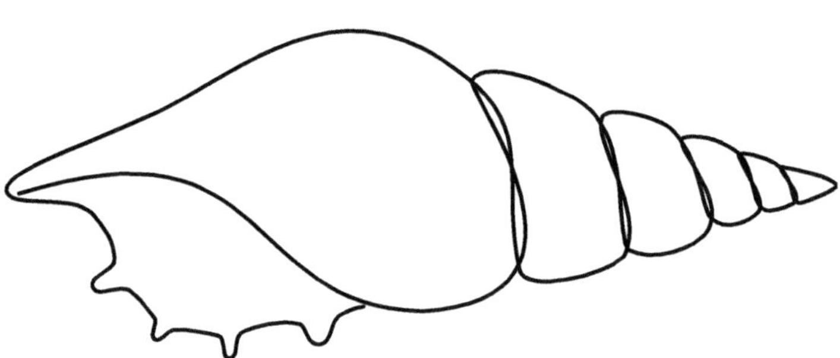

Simple Pleasures Are Life's Treasures

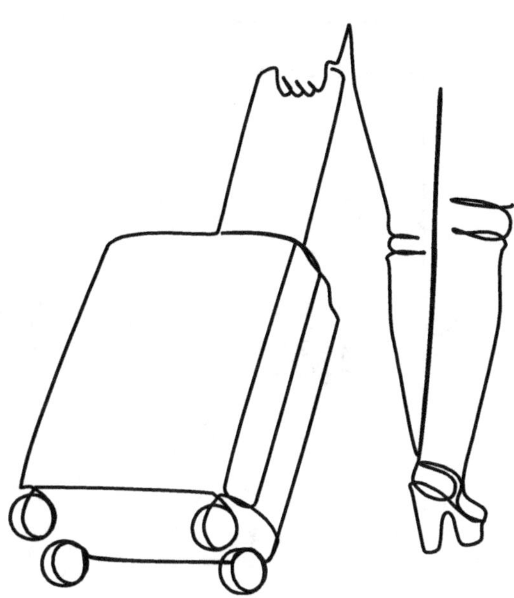

Open Yourself Up to Life's Experiences

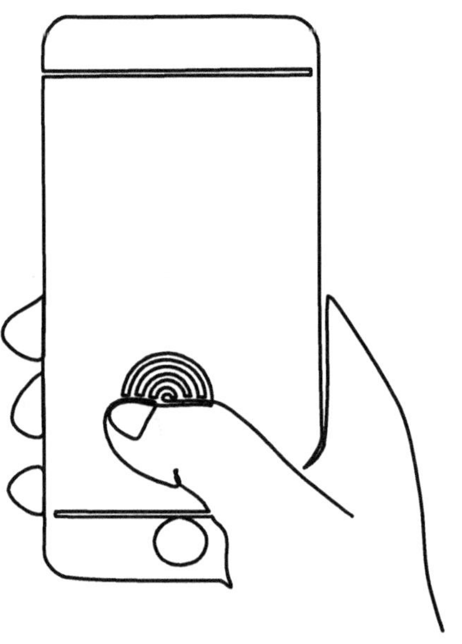

You Are Unique

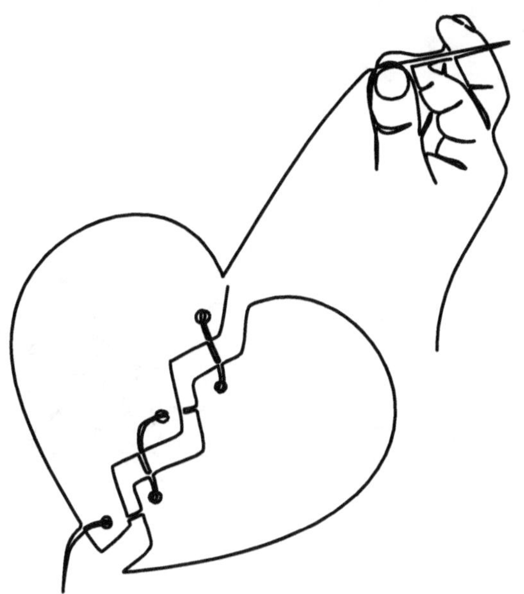

You Are in Control of How You Heal

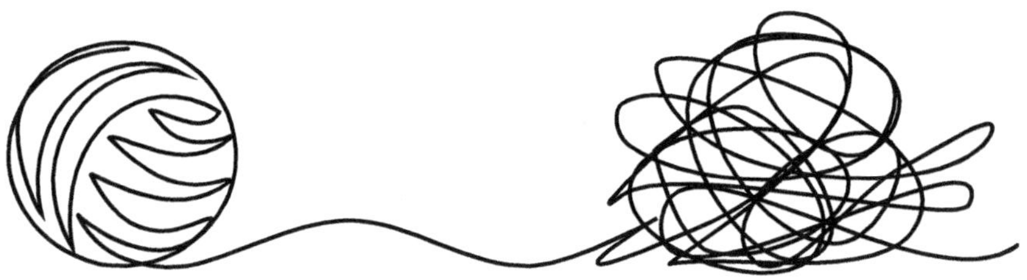

Keep Your World Simple

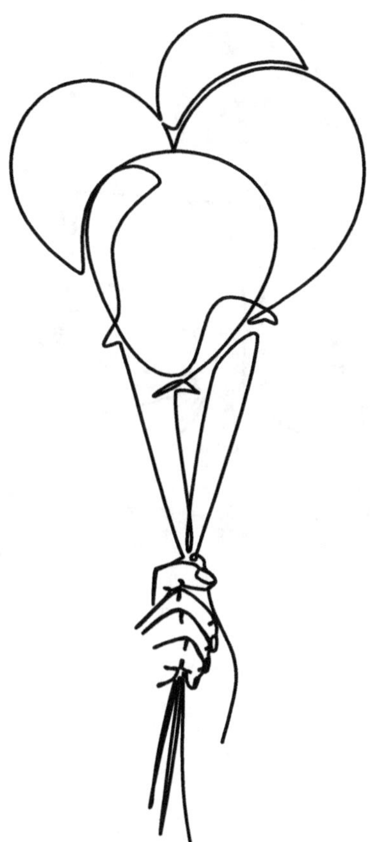

Learn When to Hold On and When to Let Go

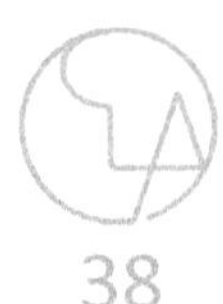

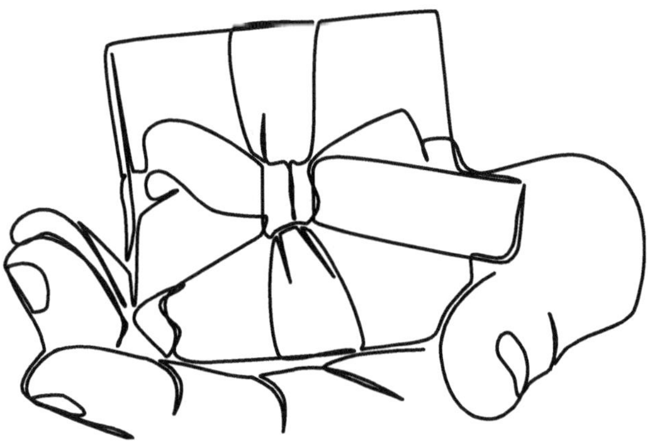

Being in the Present Is the Best Gift We Can Have

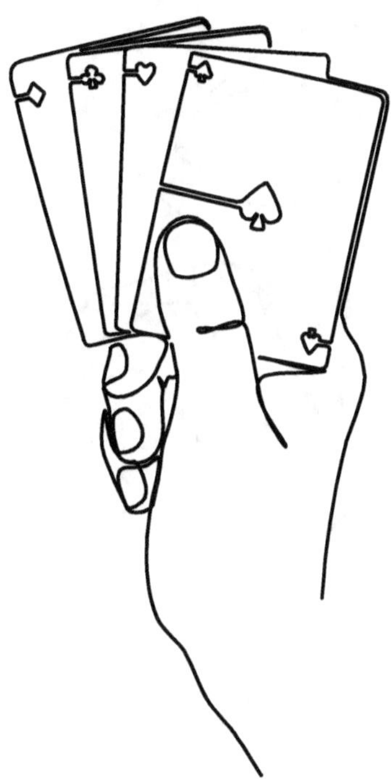

Life Is About Loving the Game, Not Winning or Losing

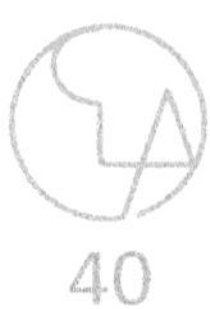

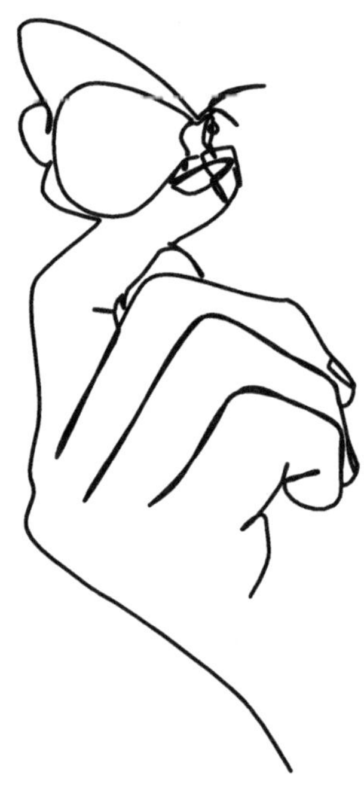

Going Through Hardships Helps Us Evolve

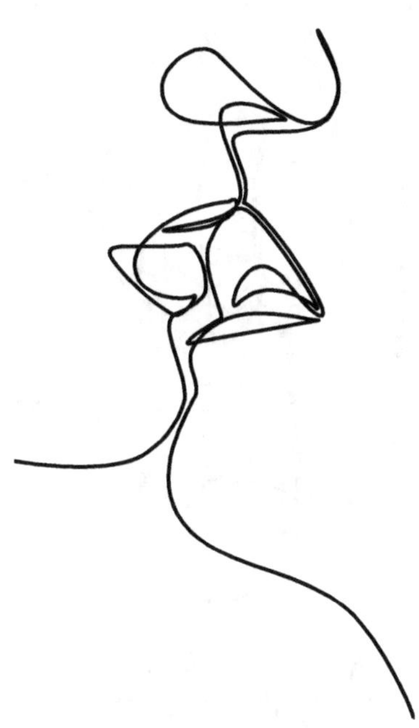

Nurture Your Relationships

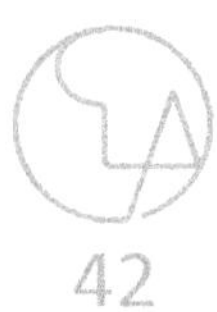

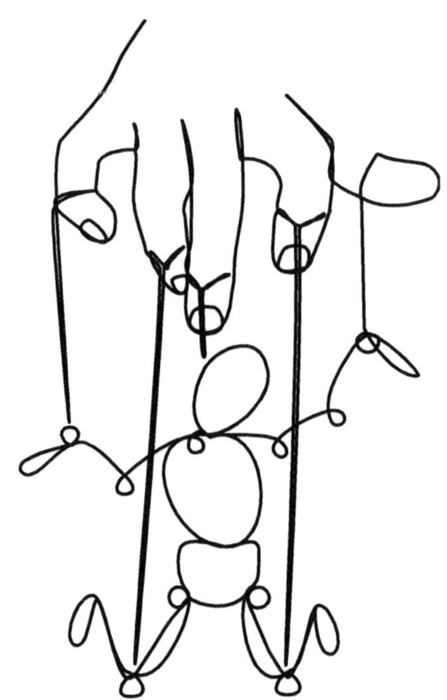

Be the Master of Your Own Thoughts

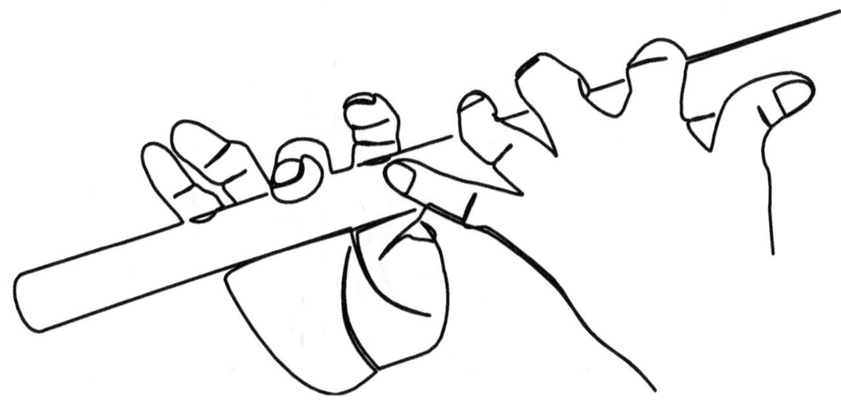

Live in Harmony with Yourself

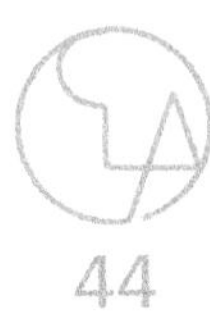

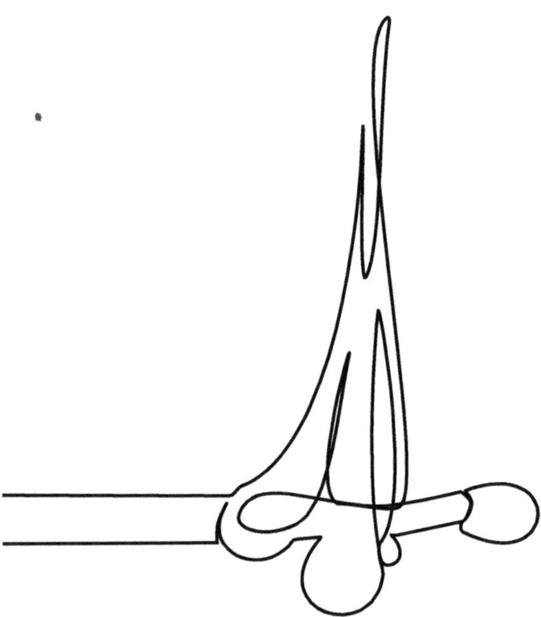

Don't Let Anyone Put Out the Fire Inside You

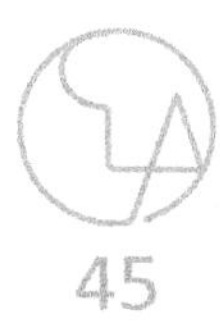

45

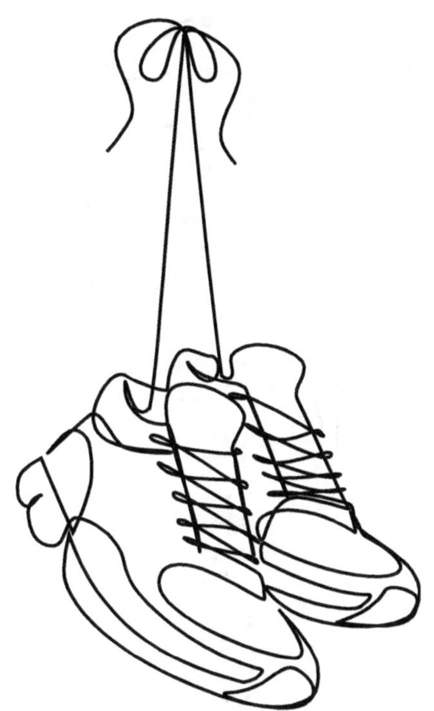

No Pain, No Gain

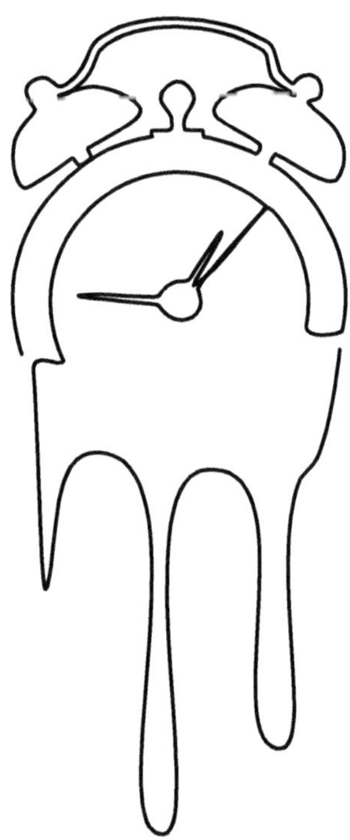

Value Your Time

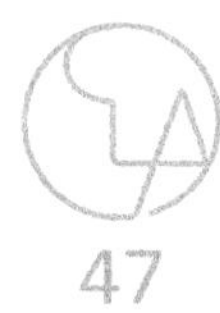

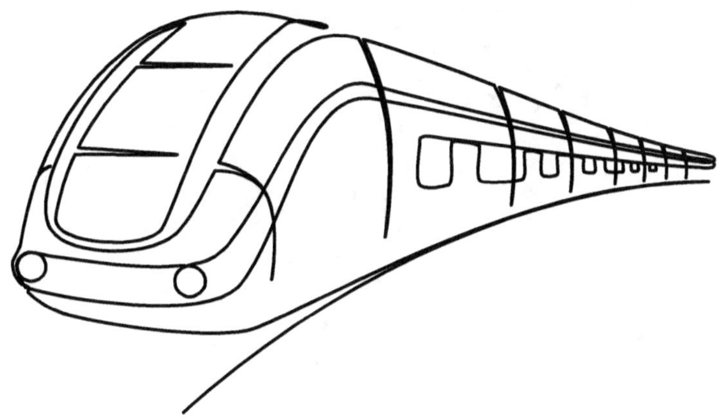

Make the Most of the Ride

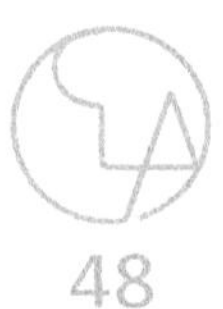

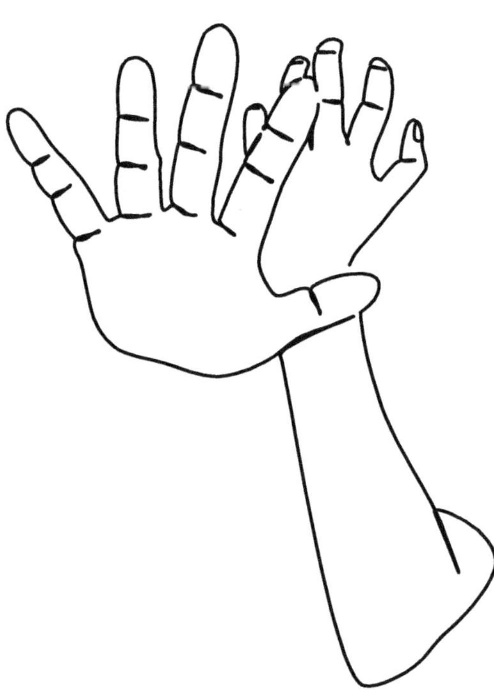

Make the Journey from Fear to Faith

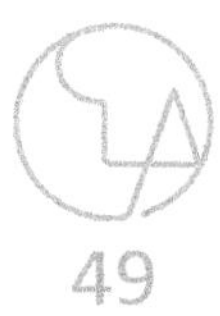

49

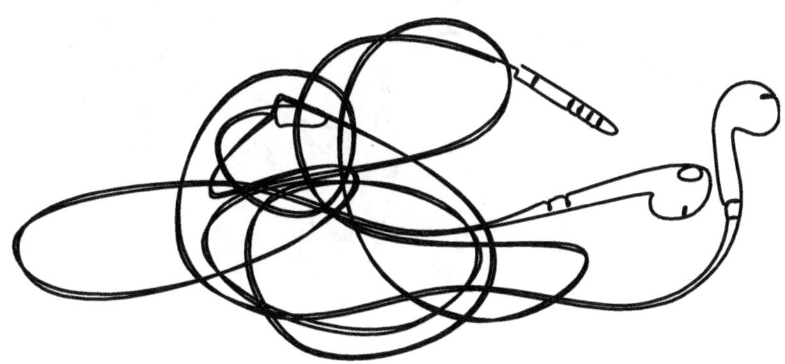

Untangle Your Mind

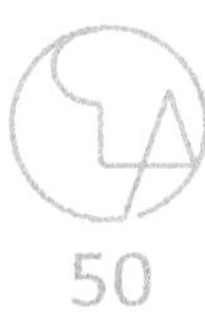

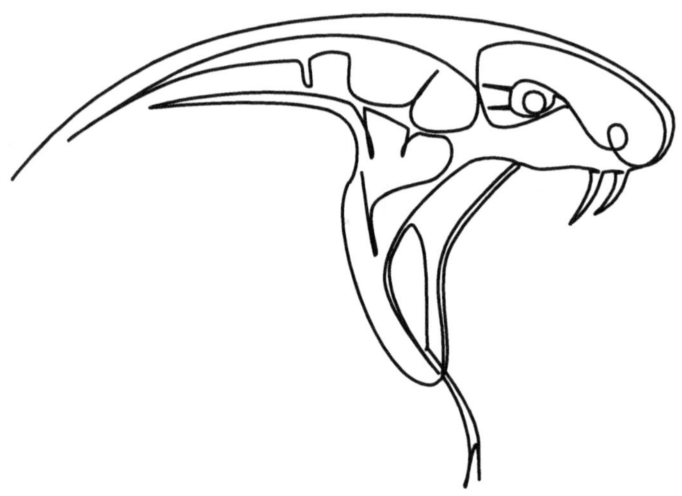

Don't Let Others Poison You

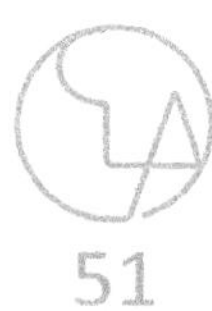

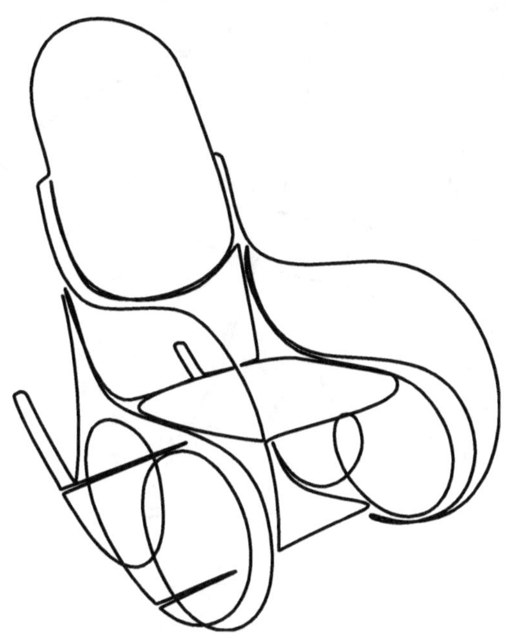

Worrying Won't Get You Anywhere

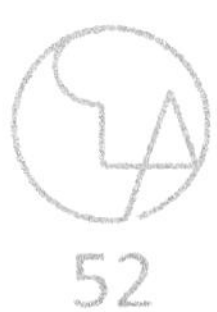

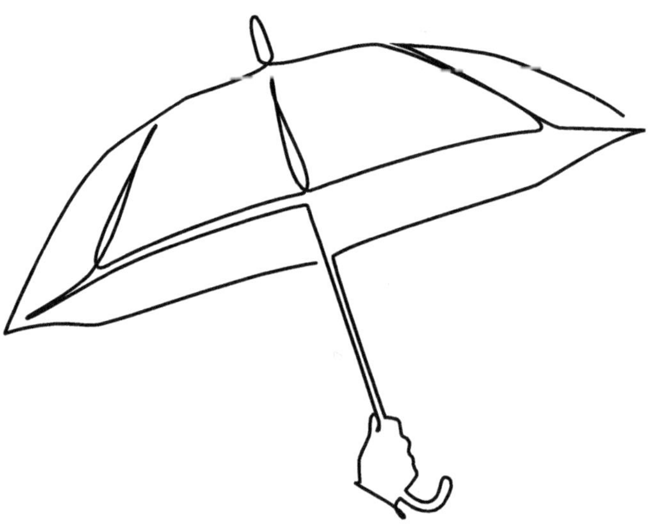

The Mind Functions Best When Open

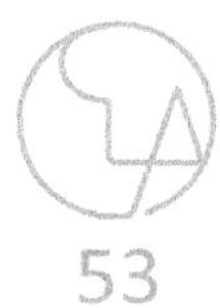

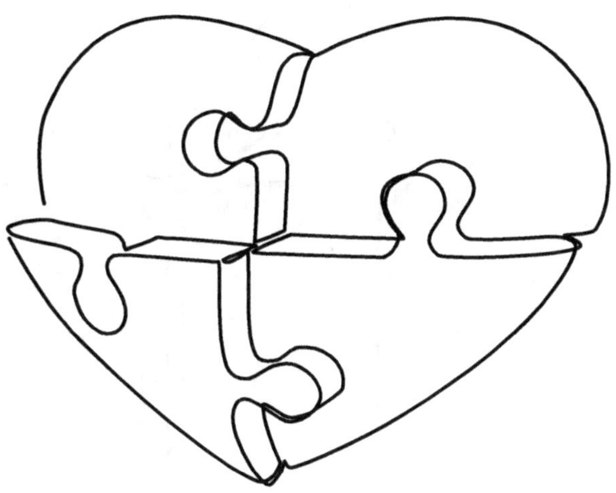

Build Love Until the End

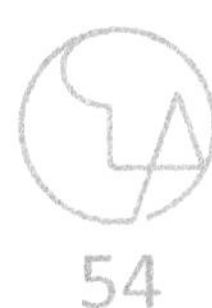

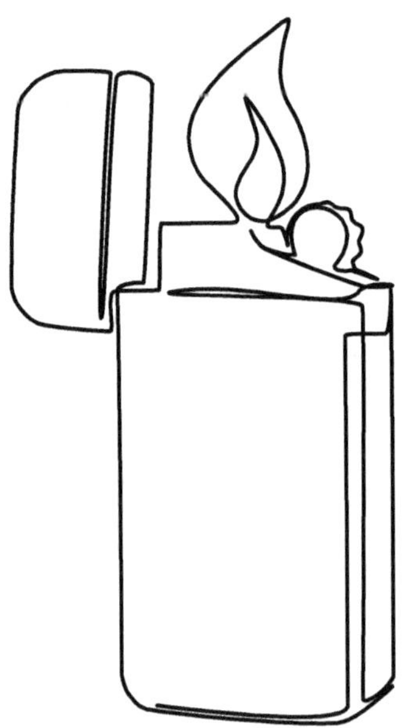

Don't Burn Yourself Out Looking After Other People

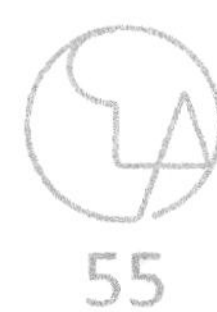

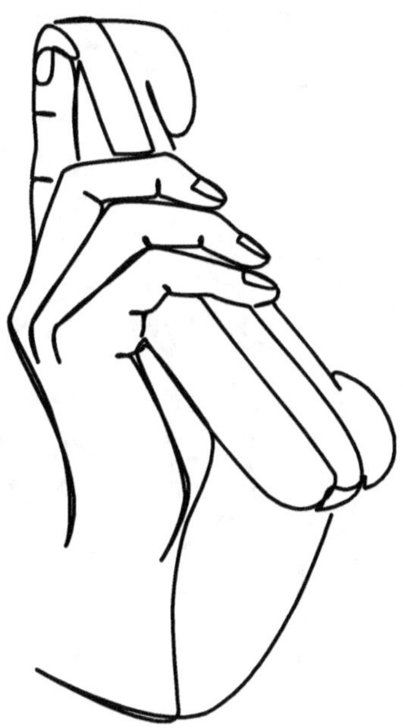

We Are in Charge of Our Attitudes

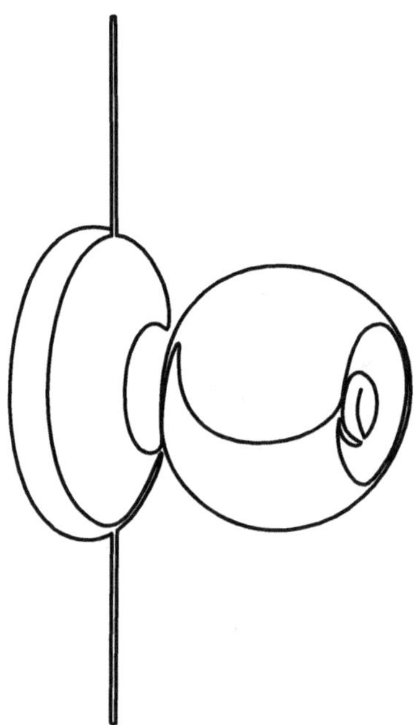

As One Door Closes, Another Opens

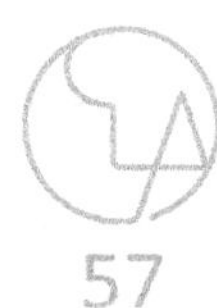

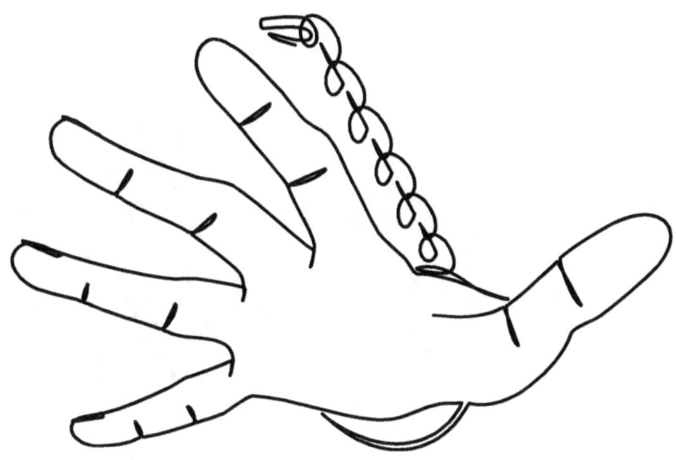

We Don't Appreciate What We Have Until It's Gone

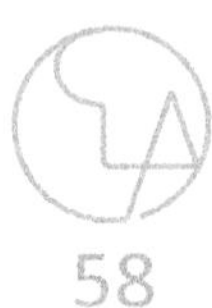

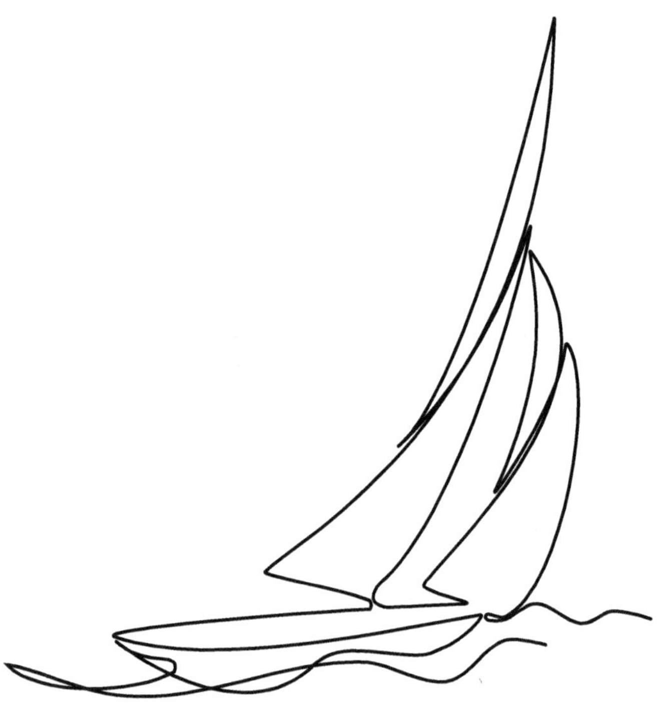

A Smooth Sea Never Made a Skilled Sailor

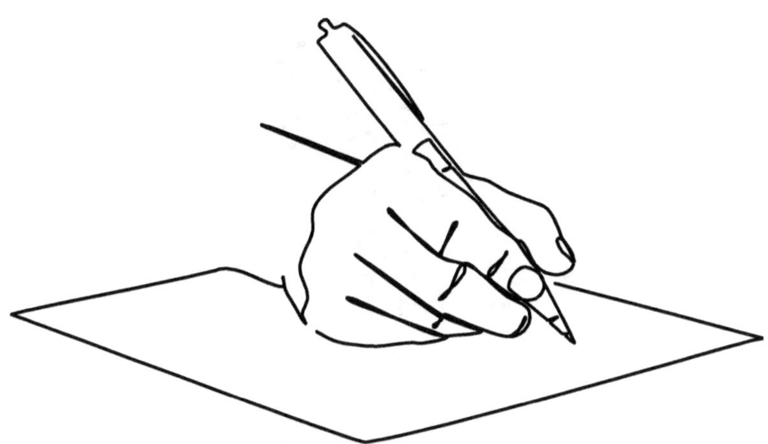

Every Day of Your Life Is a Page of Your History

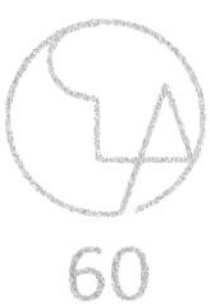

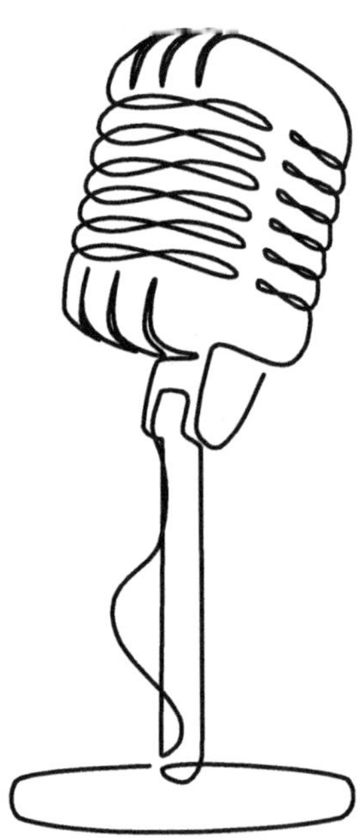

Don't Just Talk, Act

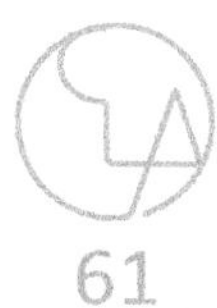

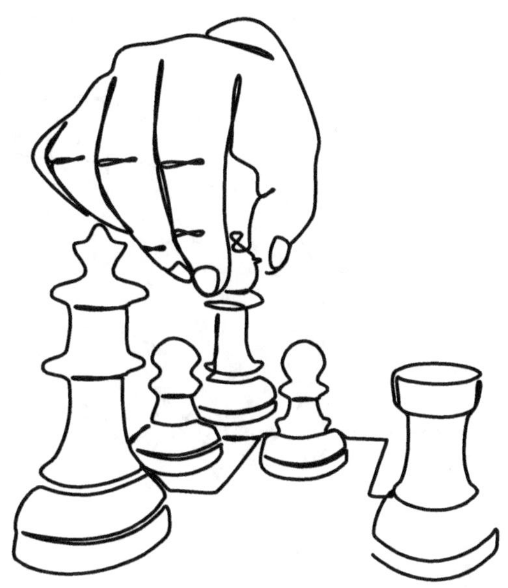

Failure Makes You Strong

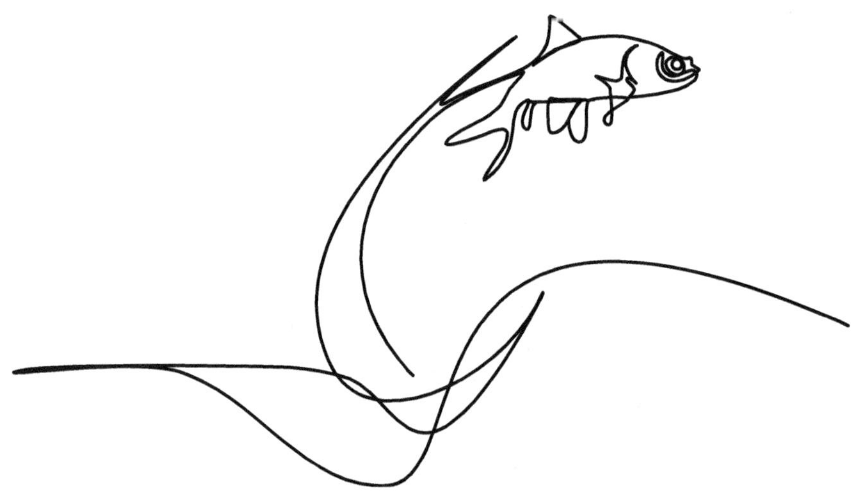

Bigger Fish Are Found Deeper in the Water

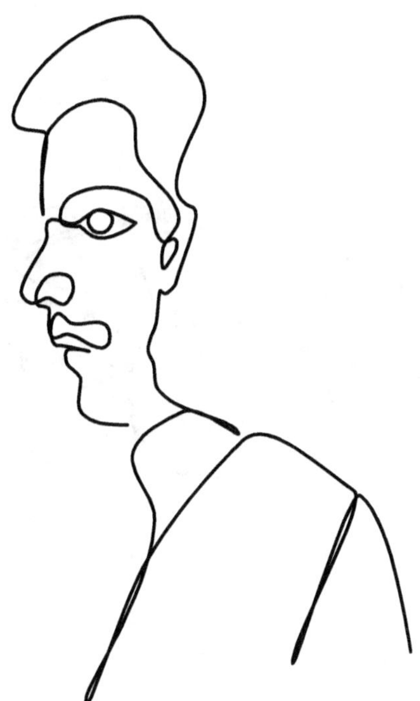

We Only See the World Through Our Own Eyes

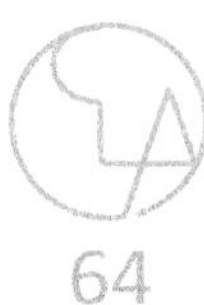

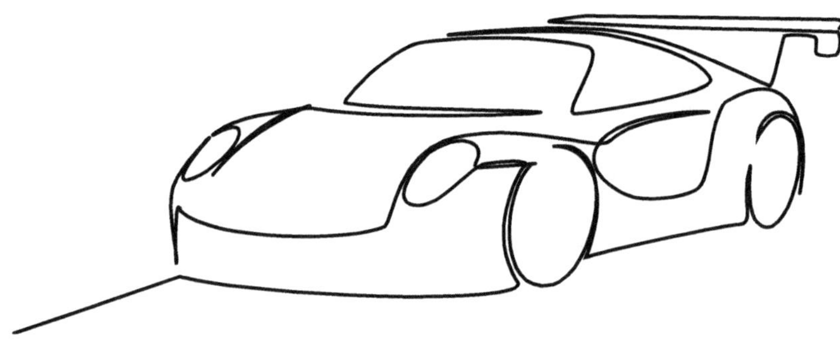

The Winner Is the One Who Refuses to Lose

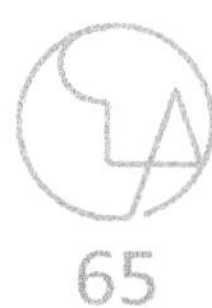

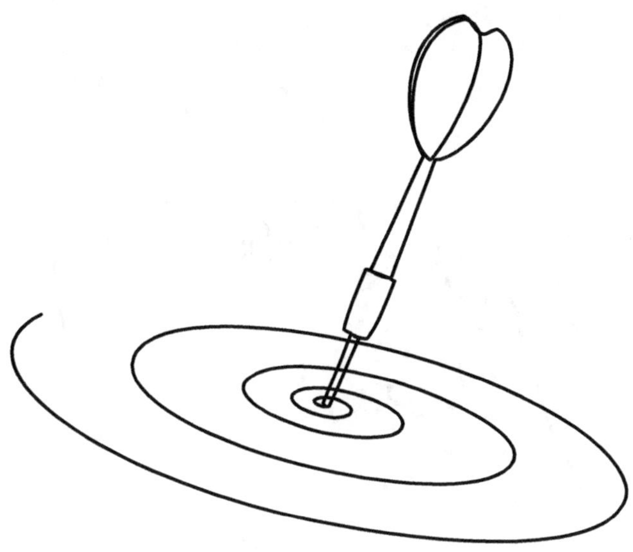

Stay Focused on Your Goals

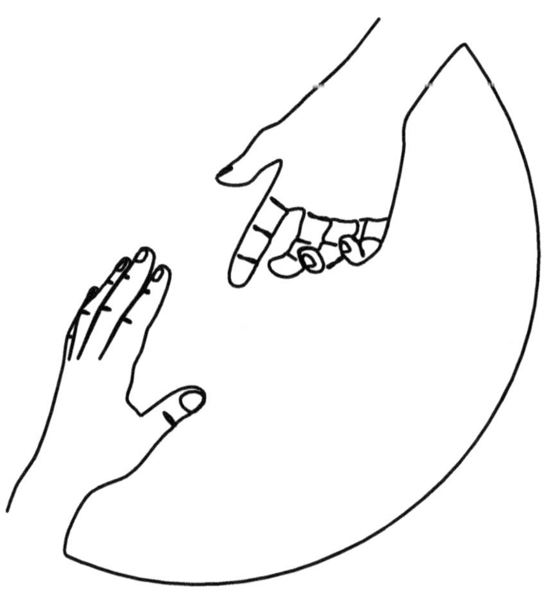

May We Help More Than We Hurt

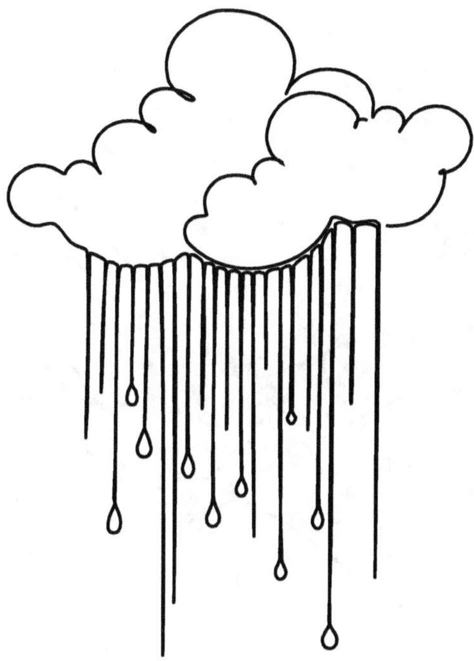

Every Cloud Has a Silver Lining

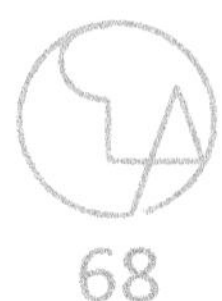

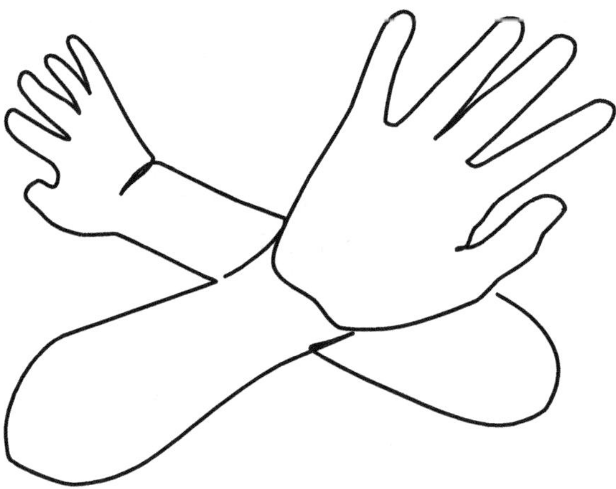

Love Yourself Enough to Set Boundaries

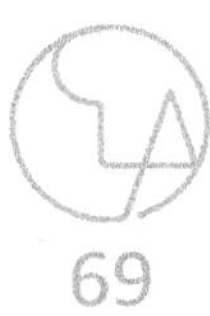

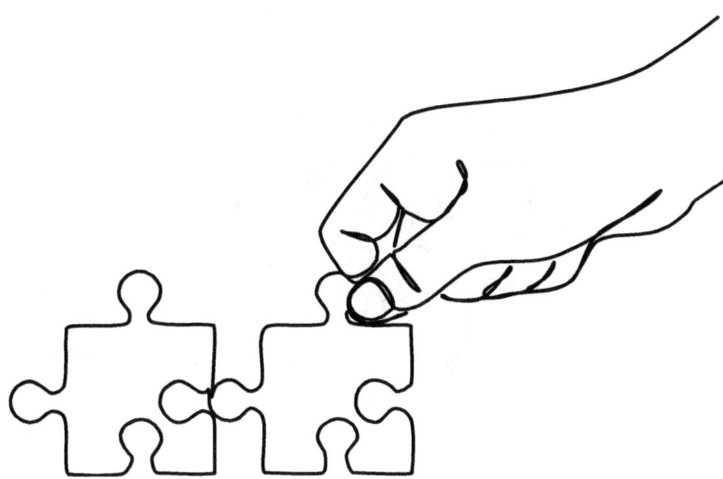

You Are Unique

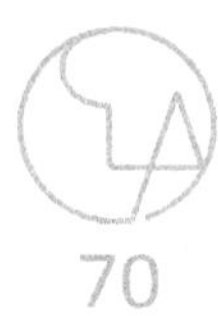

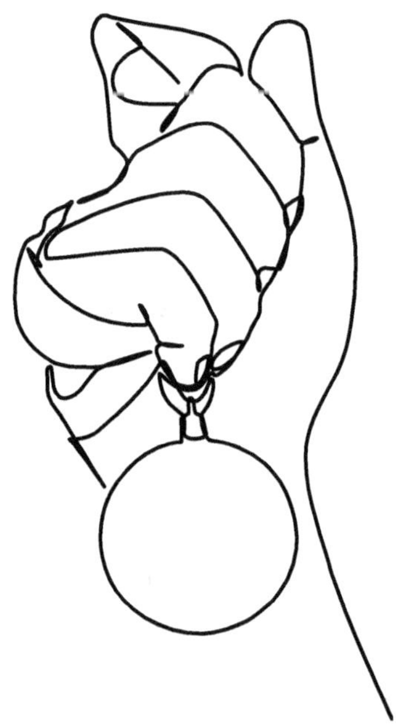

Success Is the Sum of Small Repeated Efforts

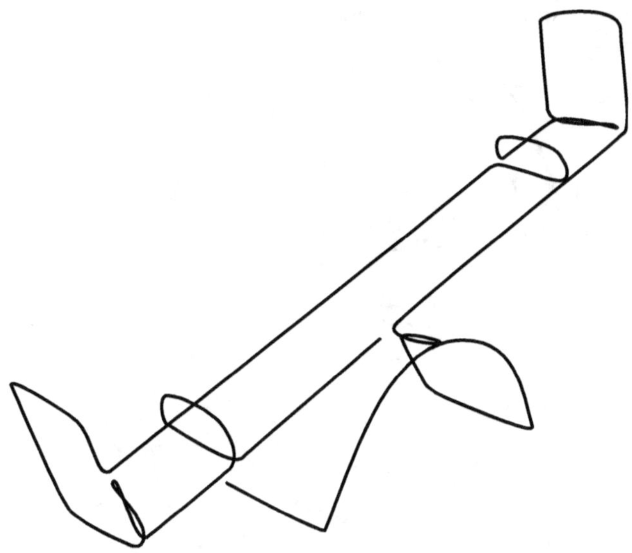

Balance Your Thoughts with Actions

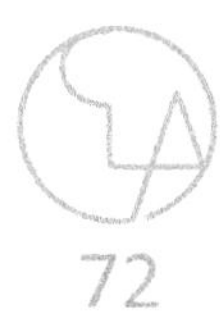

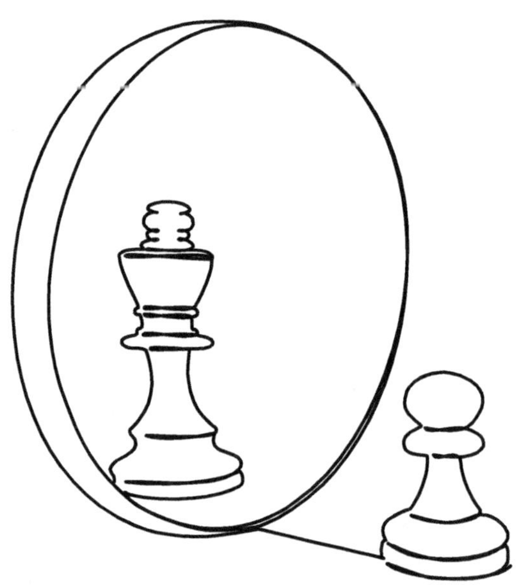

Have the Courage to Pursue Your Dreams

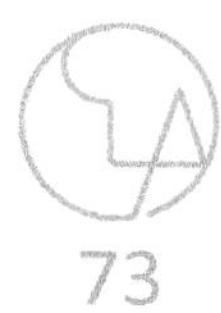

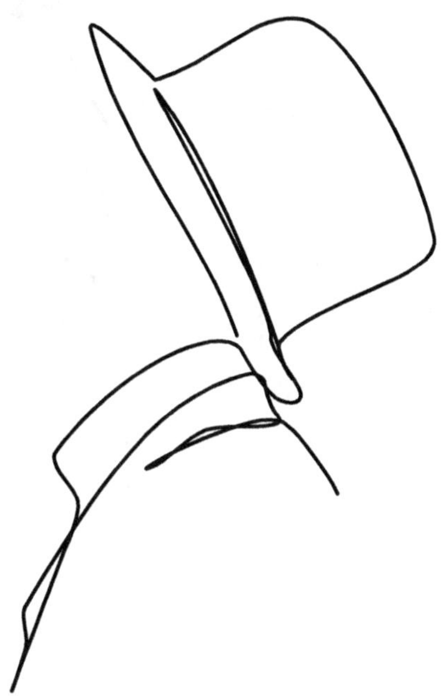

Be Your Genuine Self

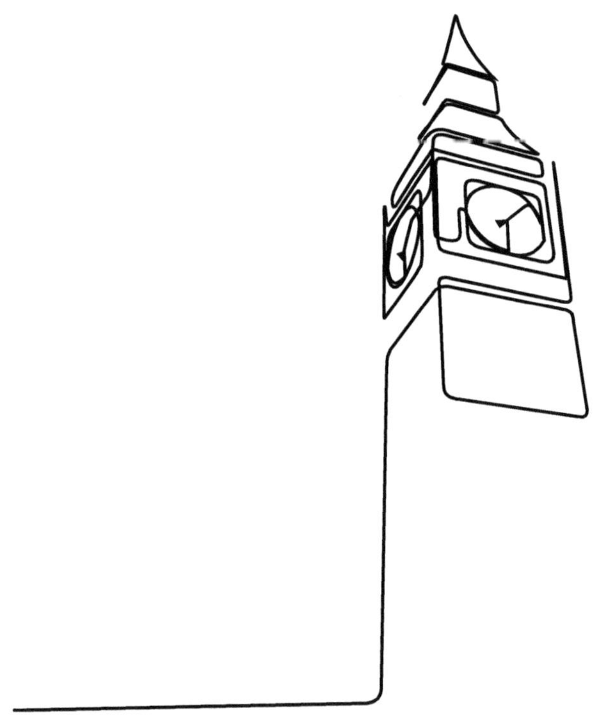

Time Is Life

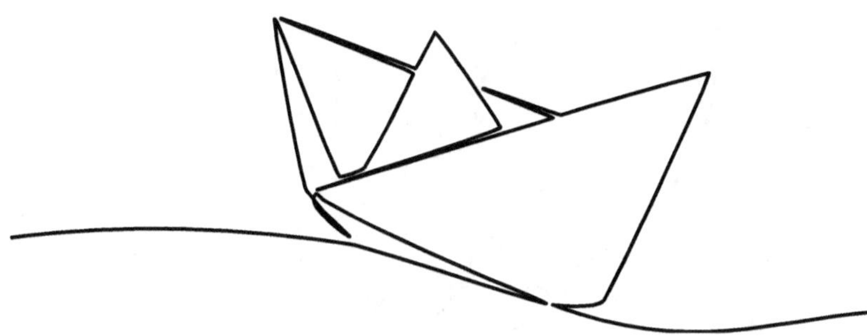

We Are Shaped by Our Environments, but We Can Rise Above

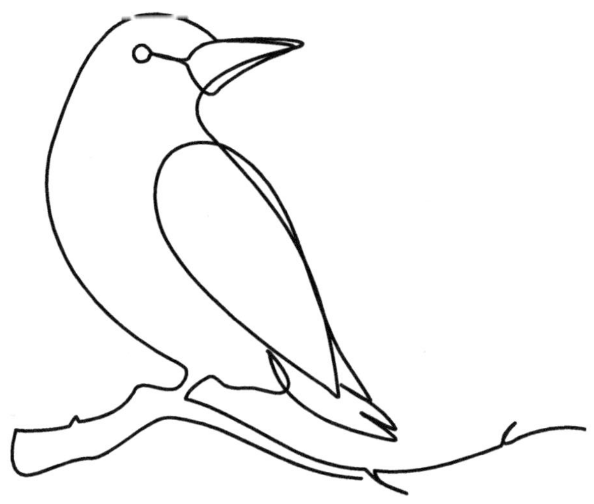

Have Faith in Your Own Abilities

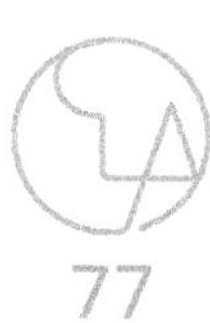

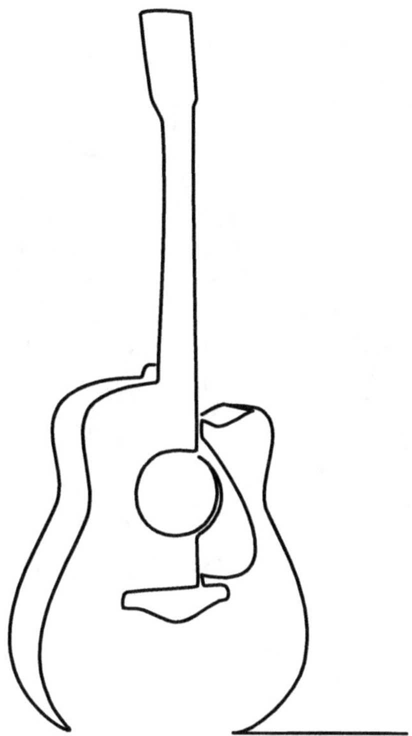

Don't Live and Die with Your Music Unplayed

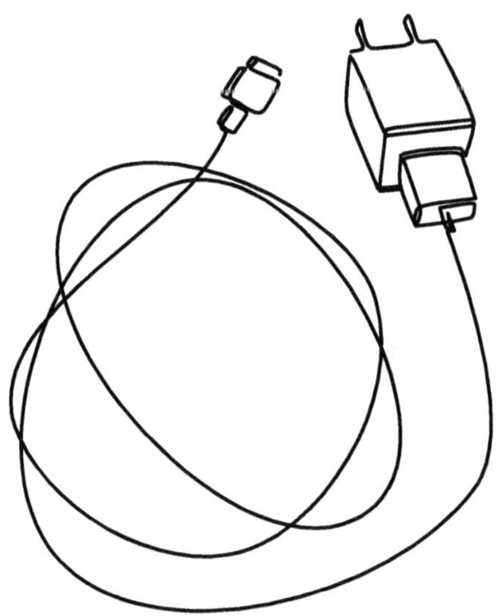

Take Time to Recharge

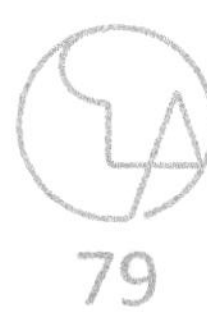

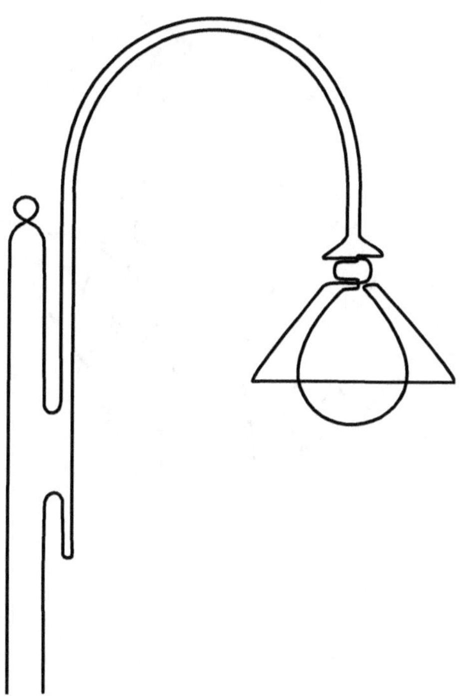

Let Your Inner Light Guide You

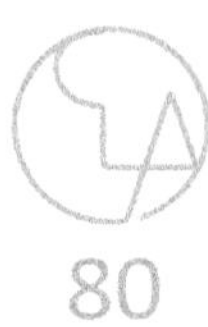

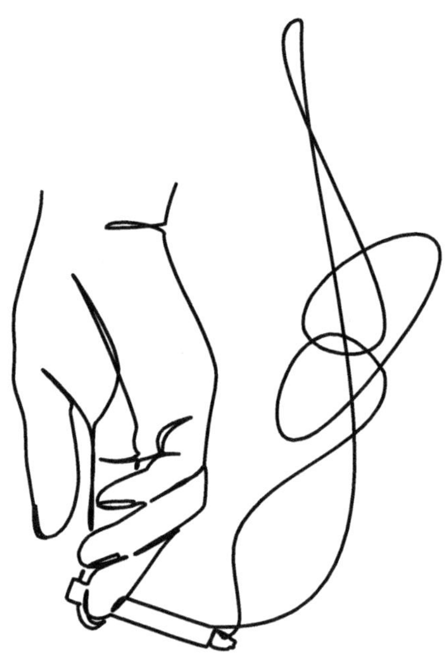

A Problem Shared Is a Problem Halved

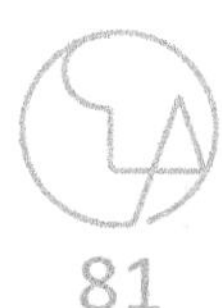

81

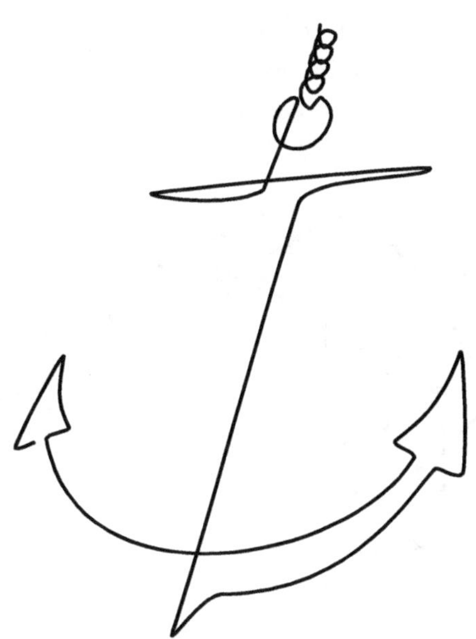

Don't Let Anything Hold You Back from What You Want

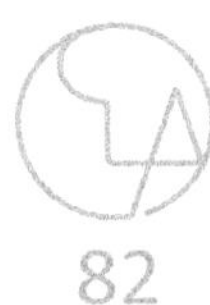

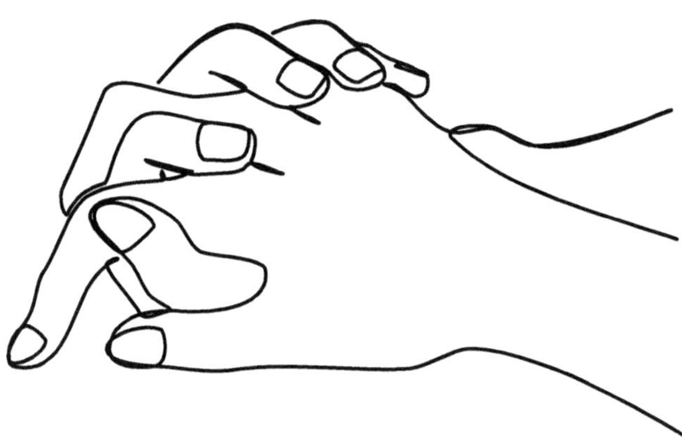

Let Love Be the Essence of All Relationships

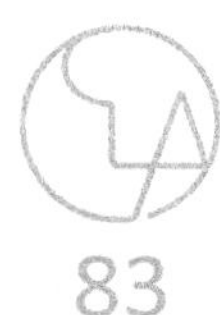

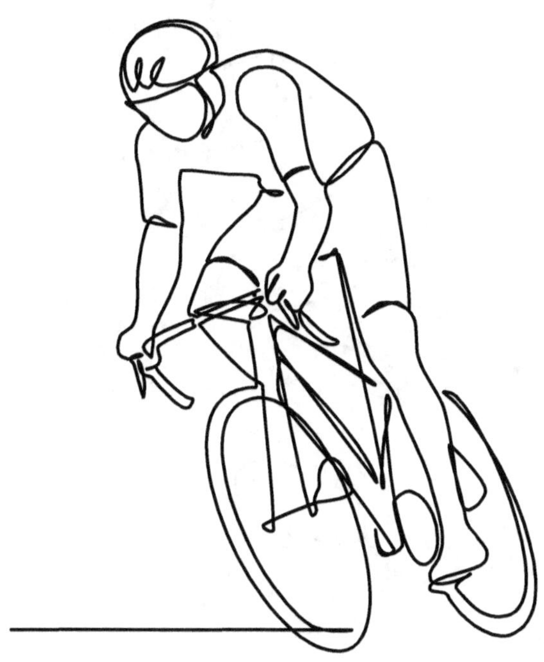

To Keep Your Balance, You Must Keep Moving

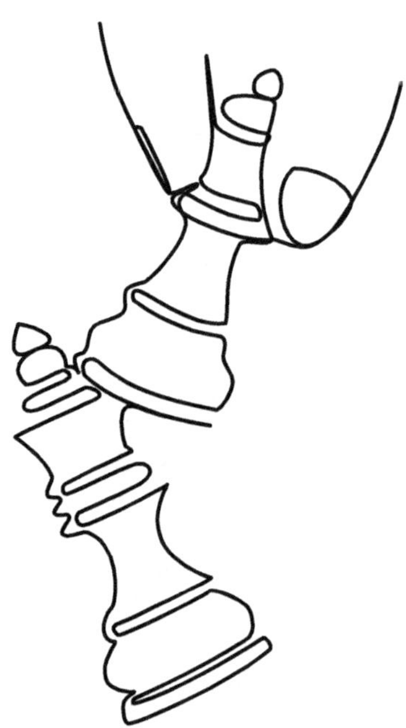

Losing Is a Blueprint for Winning

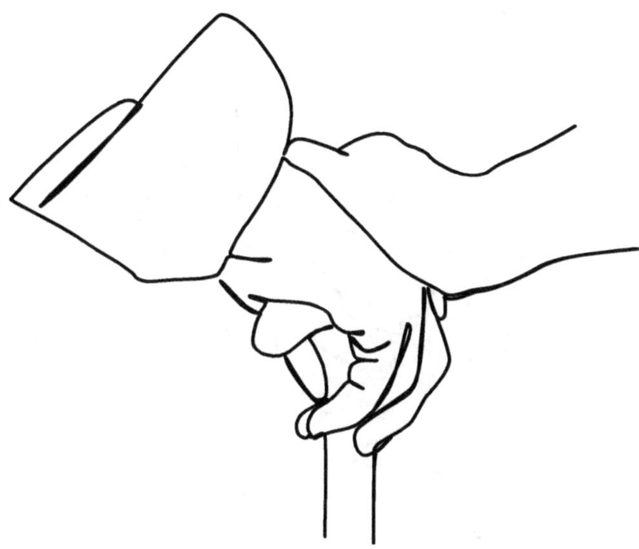

You're Only as Old as You Think You Are

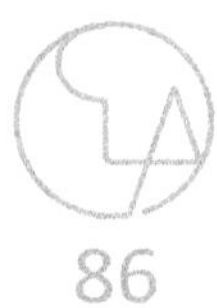

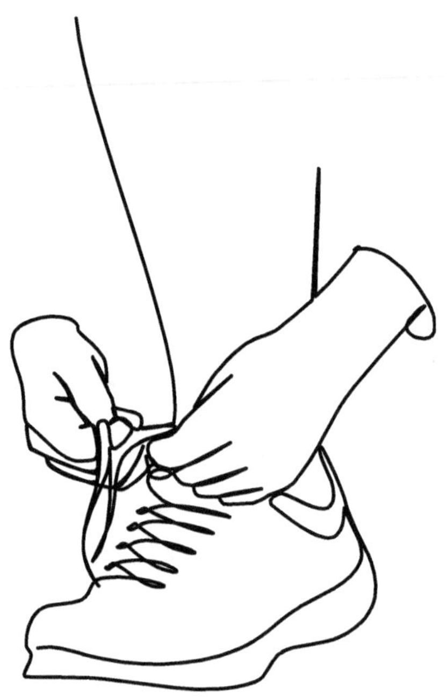

Every Journey Begins with a Single Step

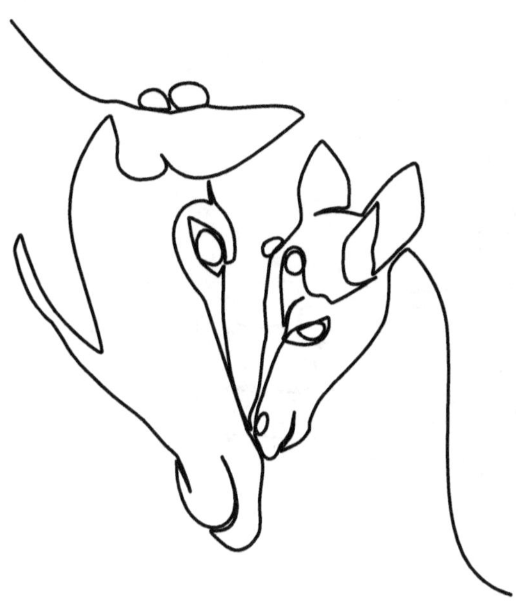

Some Things Are Infinite

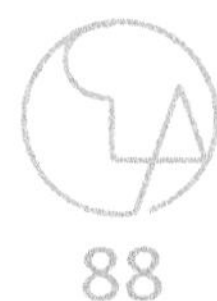

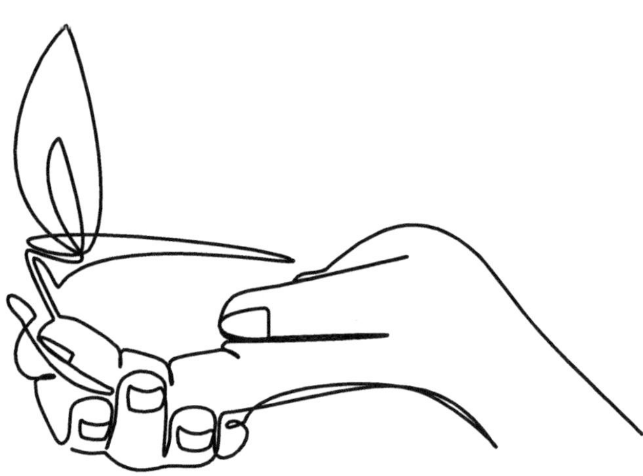

Better to Light a Candle Than to Curse the Darkness

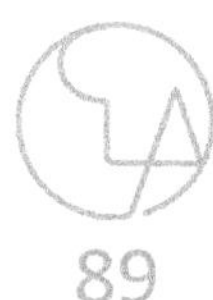

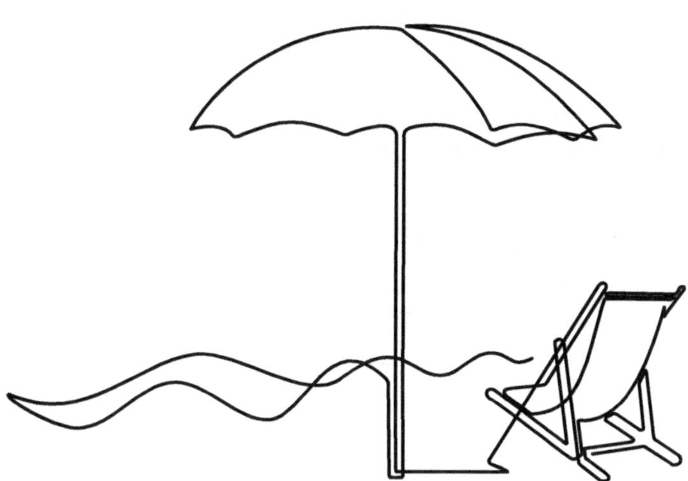

Taking the Wheel of the Ship in a Calm Sea Is Easy

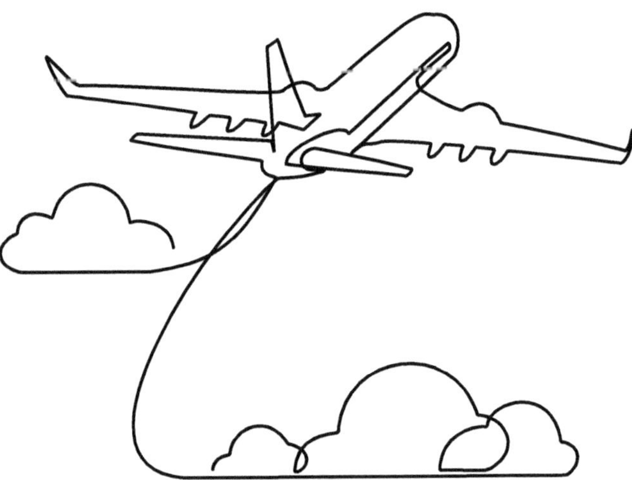

An Airplane Takes Off Against Gravity, Not With It

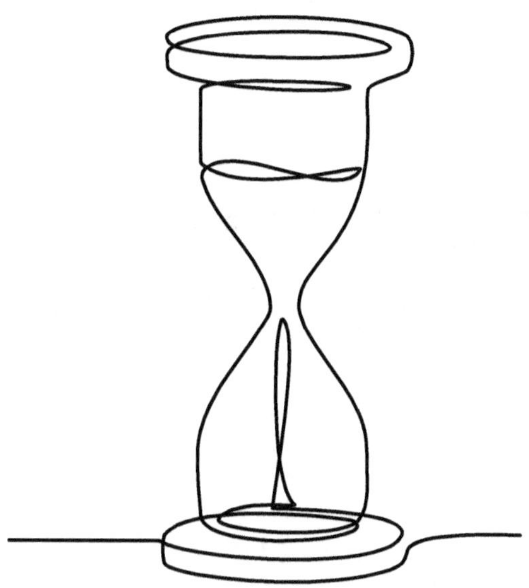

Time Alone Doesn't Change Things

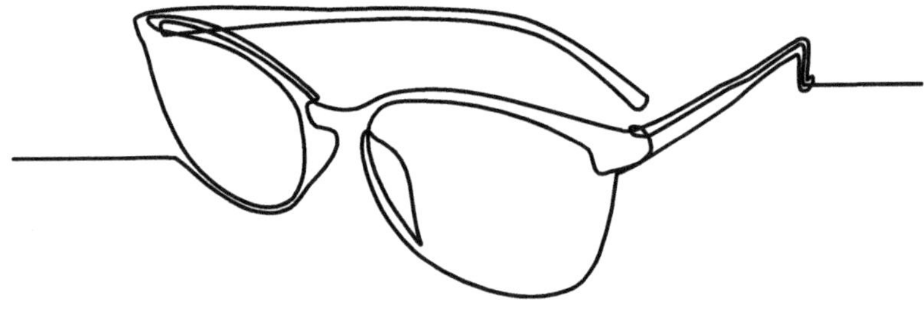

Change the Way You Look at Things

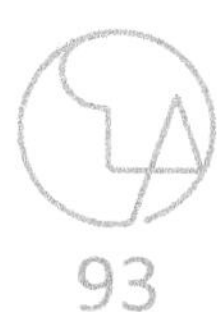

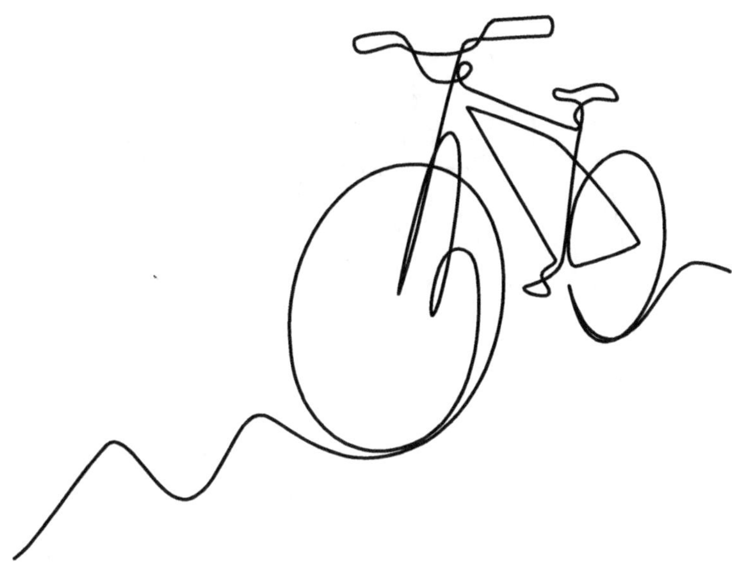

The Road to Success Is Paved with Sacrifices and Determination

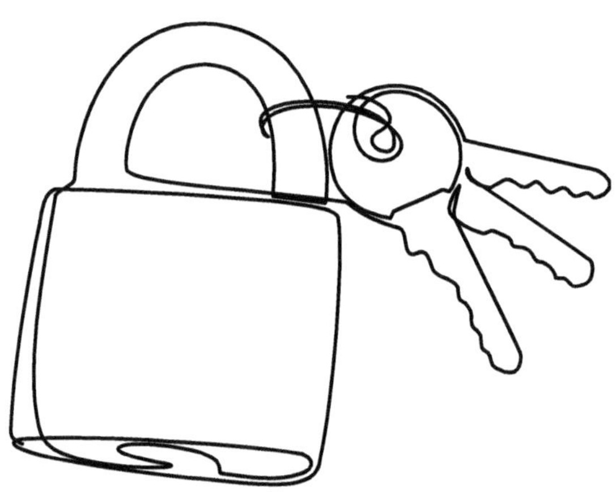

Every Problem Has Its Solution

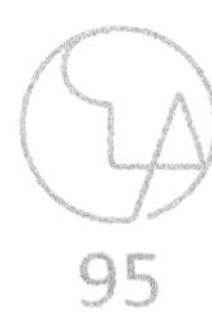

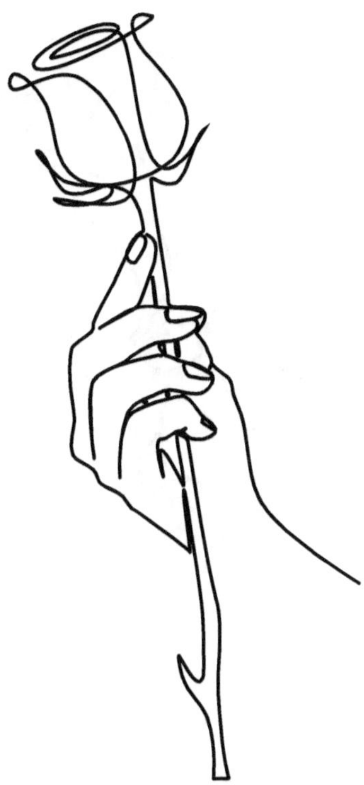

It Is Not the Thorns That People See but the Rose

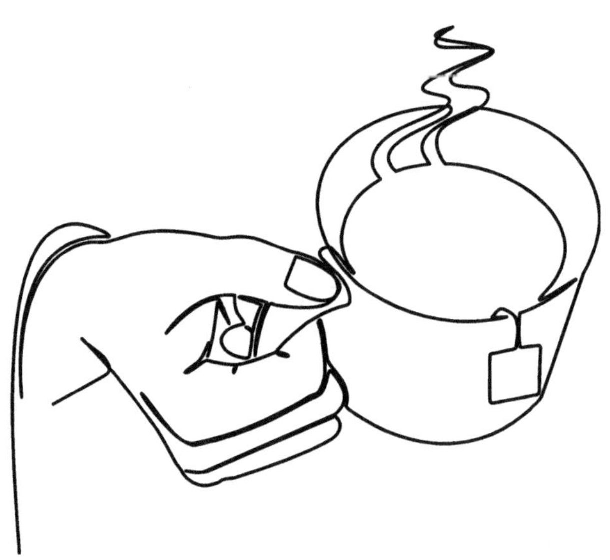

Put Yourself in Hot Water and You Will Know Your Strength

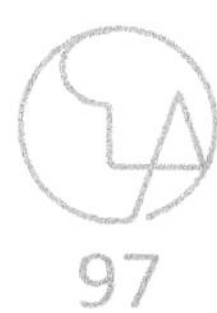

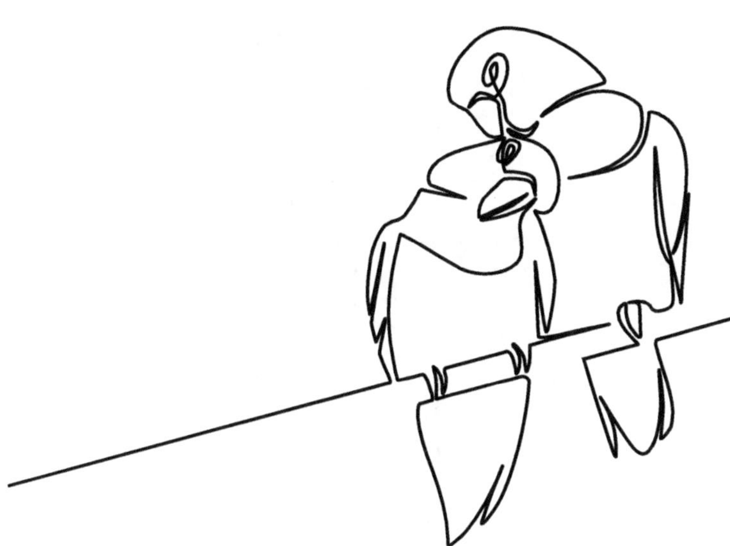

Are We Getting and Giving Enough Love?

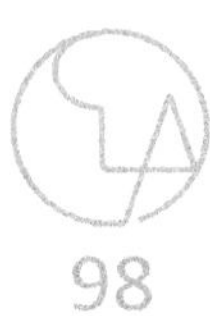

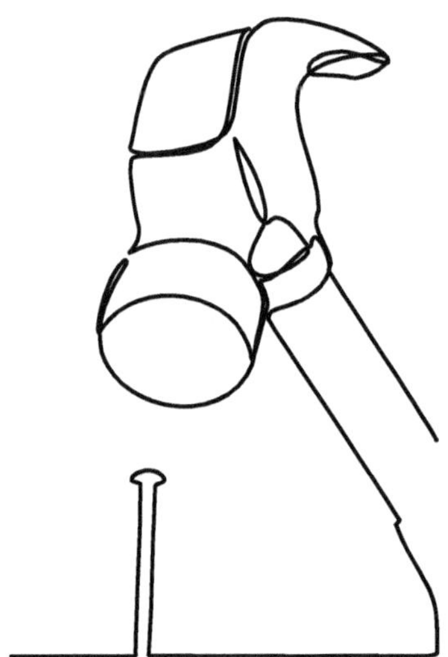

Your Character Is a Product of a Thousand Strokes

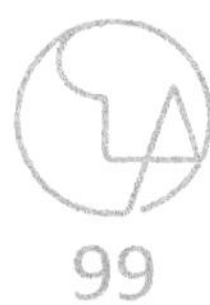

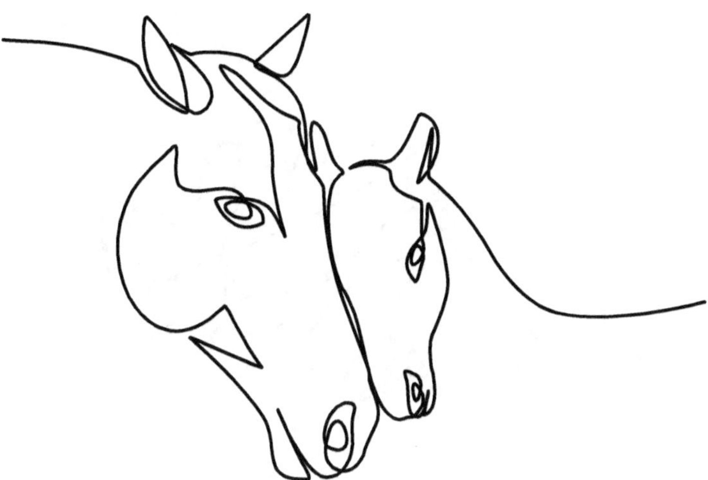

Love to Love, Not to Be Loved

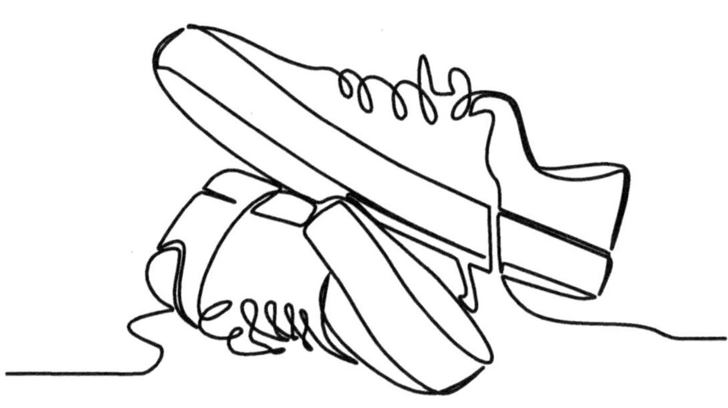

The Journey Matters More than the Destination